The Bloomsbury Anthology of

GREAT INDIAN POEMS

Also by Abhay K.

The Seduction of Delhi
CAPITALS
100 Great Indian Poems
100 More Great Indian Poems
The Eight-eyed Lord of Kathmandu

The Bloomsbury Anthology of GREAT INDIAN POEMS

Edited by

Abhay K.

B L O O M S B U R Y

NEW DELHI • LONDON • OXFORD • NEW YORK • SYDNEY

BLOOMSBURY INDIA
Bloomsbury Publishing India Pvt Ltd
Second Floor, LSC Building No. 4, DDA Complex, Pocket C – 6 & 7,
Vasant Kunj, New Delhi 110070

BLOOMSBURY, BLOOMSBURY INDIA and the Diana logo are trademarks of Bloomsbury Publishing Plc

First published 2019

ISBN: 978-93-89449-57-0

2 4 6 8 10 9 7 5 3 1

Printed and bound in India by Replika Press Pvt Ltd

To find out more about our authors and books
visit www.bloomsbury.com and sign up for our newsletters

CONTENTS

EDITOR'S NOTE

On 10 December 1950, William Faulkner began his Nobel Prize acceptance speech with these words, 'I feel that this award was not made to me as a man, but to my work – a life's work in the agony and sweat of the human spirit, not for glory and least of all for profit...' As art transcends the artist, poetry transcends the poet. Faulkner further elaborated upon the importance of artwork over the artist in an interview with The Paris Review in 1956. Referring to the futility of conflict over the authorship of Shakespeare's works, he contends, '...what is important is *Hamlet* and *A Midsummer Night's Dream*, not who wrote them, but that somebody did. The artist is of no importance. Only what he creates is important.'

This is what I had in mind when I started editing *100 Great Indian Poems* and its companion volume *100 More Great Indian Poems*, which combined together make *The Bloomsbury Anthology of Great Indian Poems*. The poetry anthologies I had come across while growing up in India had a clear emphasis on 'the poets,' which is illustrated in the titles such as *Ten Twentieth Century Indian Poets*, *Twelve Modern Indian Poets, Nine Indian Women Poets* or *60 Indian Poets*. An exception may be *These My Words*, edited by Eunice de Souza and Melanie Silgardo, which could be otherwise daunting and inaccessible to common people. These lines from De Souza's poem 'Meeting Poets' are telling–

I am disconcerted sometimes
by the colour of their socks
the suspicion of a wig
the wasp in the voice
and an air, sometimes, of dankness.
Best to meet in poems:
cool speckled shells
in which one hears
a sad but distant sea

A general reader does not need to know which prizes a poet has won, how many books has s/he published or which festivals has s/he attended; the charm and force of an individual poem is sufficient to move the reader. Poetry survives the poets because of its timeless and intrinsic value. Therefore, I don't understand the obsession of the 20th century anthologists of Indian poetry with the poets.

I was fascinated with *Rashmirathi* by Ramdhari Singh Dinkar while growing up as a child in rural Bihar. I chanced upon my father's worn-out copy of this book at home when I was in class four. The magic that I had felt in the sound and energy of words in *Rashmirathi* stays with me till date. This Hindi epic tells the story of Karna, Krishna, Pandavas and Kauravas. It was my first lesson in literature as well as in politics and diplomacy. I memorized its third canto by heart as I often read it. I still do. I have unsuccessfully tried to translate this work into English. The magic of native words is lost in translation; and therefore, verses from *Rashmirathi* do not find a place in the anthology of great Indian poems. For the similar reason of untranslatability, several other great poems could not fit into this anthology.

My desire to take *rasa* and riches of Indian poetry to the world and to bring the focus back to the poem from the poet gave birth to *100 Great Indian Poems*. This was called for after having brought some of the world's best poems to India in *CAPITALS* in 2017. It received overwhelming reception in India and abroad. Its first volume sold out within first few months of its publication.

Commenting on the selection of poems in *100 Great Indian Poems*, French philosopher Christopher Macann said, 'they are quintessential, always simple, often profound, generously sensuous, occasionally political and frequently funny.' Reviewing the anthology in the First Post, Manik Sharma wrote, '*100 Great Indian Poems* attempts something endearingly unique and preposterously impossible—to merge and collate 3000 years of Indian poetry's history via a hundred of its samplings...'

100 Great Indian Poems has been translated into Portuguese, Spanish, Italian, Irish, Russian, French, Malagasy and Nepali. The Portuguese edition is published by the University of São Paulo, Brazil, the Spanish edition by the Autonomous University of Nuevo León, Monterrey, Mexico while its Italian edition is published by *Edizione Efesto* in Rome, Italy. It is for the first time that a poetry anthology from so many Indian languages covering over three thousand years of Indian poetry has been translated and published into several world languages.

The overwhelming interest of translators and readers inspired me to come up with *100 More Great Indian Poems* to serve as its companion volume, and the growing demand for both these anthologies inspired me to bring out a combined volume titled as *The Bloomsbury Anthology of Great Indian Poems*.

India has a plethora of languages and each language's rich nuance is tapped in poems waiting to be discovered, read, discussed and cherished. How does one put together an anthology of poems from so many Indian languages? How does one introduce the gems of Indian poetry to the world?

India's regional languages have a wealth of great Indian poems which rarely comes out in the absence of good translations. Every poem included in this anthology speaks out loud—we need more translations and translators. Most of the translators in this anthology are poets themselves, who carry not only a poetic but also linguistic sensitivity, the prerequisite for rendering these poems from India's regional languages effectively into English. This anthology also highlights the achievements of Indian poetry written in English by Indian poets as well as Indian diaspora poets and how they have turned English, once a foreign language, into their own.

Editing this anthology has been a labour of love. I have read widely, almost all poetry anthologies covering different languages and geographical regions of India published so far. It includes poems translated from twenty-eight Indian languages, viz., Assamese, Bengali, Bhili, Chakma, Dogri, Gondi, Gujarati, Hindi, Kannada, Kashmiri, Khasi, Kokborok, Konkani, Maithili, Malayalam, Marathi, Nepali, Oriya, Persian, Punjabi, Rajasthani, Sanskrit, Santhali, Sindhi, Tamil, Telugu, Urdu and Prakrit languages including Pali as well as poems originally written in English.

There is an abundance of light, irony, sensuousness and spirituality in the poems. But, what makes a poem an Indian poem? How is it different from an African or a Latin American poem? I think it is the smorgasbord of sensibilities, landscapes, customs, rituals and mythologies these poems concoct and offer, which are uniquely Indian in some way or the other.

The canvas of this collection covers over 3000 years of Indian poetry. Interestingly, along with many well-known names, some poets whose poems are included in the anthology are virtually unknown even in poetry circles. Poems included in this anthology have shades of all *rasas* (which roughly translates as flavours) including erotic, comic, heroic, horrific among other strains and cover almost all traditions of Indian poetry including bhakti poetry. The distinctive voices of the tribal, dalit, feminist and LGBT communities also find space in this collection.

What makes a poem great? Is there a standard definition of a great poem? I have a simple answer to this question. What moves me is great for me. What moves you is great for you. It could be a painting, a piece of music, a photograph, a poem or anything under the sun. I don't think there is or there can be a universal definition of greatness. Even Buddha, the enlightened one, advised his followers not to believe what he said without verifying it themselves, not to take his path but to find one's own. In a similar vein, I would suggest you find your own great poems. Make your own anthologies of great Indian poems.

This anthology opens with an ancient verse by poet Bhavabhuti, which, looking over its shoulder, remembers the achievements of past masters but not without offering homage to the language – the vehicle of poetic spirit all over the world. May poetry live on, and myriad languages thrive in our troubled world!

The poems in this collection are arranged in alphabetic order of their respective titles instead of the chronological dates of their publication, so as to underline the timeless nature of great poetry. There are a number of great poems I could not include because of permission issues. These include 'Self Portrait' by A.K. Ramanujan, 'Station Dog' by Arun Kolatkar, 'Night of the Scorpion' by Nissim Ezekiel, 'Postcard from Kashmir' by Agha Shahid Ali, 'The Vaiyai Poems' from Paripatal, 'Indigo' by Chitra Banerjee Divakaruni, 'One Chooses a Language' by Zulfikar Ghose, Bhagavad Gita's Chapter IX translated by Stephen Mitchell, 'In the Cemetery' by Karaikkal Ammaiyar, 'Whatever wound a man inflicts on a woman' by Vatsyayana, 'Woman' by Hira Bhansode, 'The First Book' by Amrita Pritam, 'Fear of Death' by Bhartrihari among others.

With this anthology I hope to introduce you to the rich world of Indian poetry offering the distinct tastes, smells, colours and moods of a unique and ancient civilization. I read these poems again and again, in times of joy and sorrow; and while reading these, I enter into a world of bliss. I wish you too an unforgettable journey with these great Indian poems.

Abhay K.

A LOVE POEM FROM INDIA: AUTHOR'S CONSENT

– Mahe Jabeen

right then
as poetry happens
he comes and
kisses me

trying to find meter
in the sound of his feet
I close my eyes

youth
engulfs me
thoughts
that were taking shape
lose their way
my poetic images
get mercilessly plundered

an unmasked love
kisses my naked forehead
a touch immersed in my eyes
shines provocatively
on my cheek
a look perches on the curve of my neck
and moves like a breeze

poetry freed from words
entwines us

lips publish the poem
with the author's consent

Translated from Telugu by Velcheru Narayana Rao

A MARVEL
– Anon

O Poverty
great powers
you have given me
I see
the whole world
and no one sees me

Translated from Sanskrit by W.S. Merwin and J.M. Masson

A NEW WAY OF WAITING
– Shakunt Mathur

Scolded
the old servant
for his usual slowness.
For his mischief
gave a good slap
to my darling son.

To my daughter who'd been playing
gave a dozen hankies to hem.
Ordered
the oldest
to drink more milk.
Washed
all the dirty clothes.

Flipped through a few magazines.
Darned some torn clothes.
Sewed on some new buttons.
Cleaned the machine and oiled it.

Put the cover back on with care.
Took out the half-finished sewing
and repacked it in a different way.
Wiped the cupboards in the kitchen.
Cleaned the spice jars.

And still
he hasn't come home from the office.

Translated from Hindi by Aruna Sitesh and Arlene Zide

A POEM
– Mir Taqi Mir

Love brings tiny sweat into your hair
like stars marching in the dead of night.

Joy fills my eyes, remembering your hair, with tears,
    and these tears roll and shine;
Into my thoughts is woven a dark night with raindrops
    and the rolling and shining of love songs.

Translated from Urdu by E. Powys Mathers

A POEM NEVER SAYS ANYTHING

– Uttaran Chaudhuri

A poem never says anything.
It just opens a door, quietly.

Sleepless and bent
just like my aged father
waiting for me in a lonely winter night.

Translated from Bengali by the poet

AFTER THE CURFEW
– Nida Fazli

It is morning
the sky humbly bows
its head to the earth
for children are going to school

Bathing itself in the stream
the sun dons itself
in a turban of spun gold
and stands smiling by the road
for children are going to school

Winds sing out blessings
on verdant green branches
jingles by fragrant flowers
wake up the sleepy paths
the shady peepal from its
corner of the old street
waves out its hands
for children are going to school

Angles of light come out
every trail is sparkling
at this moment
every pore of the earth
throbs like a mother's heart
time sits happily
on a rundown rooftop
flying pigeons in the sky
for children are going to school
children are going to school.

Translated from Urdu by Nirupama Dutt

AGAIN SNOWFALL
– Jiban Namdung

A poet who used to write
Poems of snow
This year went to the capital
To recite the poems of snow
It is not known
When he will return to the hills
Because the snowfall has started again,
Roads are empty
Paths and corners are desolate
Walking down the same roads and paths
The poet had walked to the hot plains
In search of him, a poem has set out alone
In the snowfall this year.

Translated from Nepali by Jas Yonjan 'Pyasi'

ALPHABETS

– Nabaneeta Dev Sen

When night falls
I search for him
I bring him home
I look him in the eye
And I cage
Language.

When day breaks
Once again the world
Wraps around my eyes
And off he flies
Taking each word
That alphabet bird

Translated from Bengali by Nandana Sen

AMBAPALI
– Vishwanath Prasad Tiwari

This dense leafy mango grove
fragrant with new blossom
is not real – it will not last Ambapali
That's what Tathagat had said.
These leaves, green like parakeet feathers
shall fall,
bare branches will wither
Birds shall no longer be drawn here –
Tathagat had said.
Ambapali looks in the mirror
and asks of her gorgeous eyes, bright as gems –
She asks of her tender curls, black as swarm of bees
She asks of her arched eyebrows,
She asks of her fragrant, ornament-adorned body
She asks the trembling desires on her lips,
She asks the glowing embers of her being –
Asks Ambapali –
Can't these words of the truthful Tathagat
not be otherwise?

Ambapali: A famous royal courtesan of the Vaishali Republic in India around 500 BCE.
Tathagat: The honorific title by which Buddha is addressed.

Translated from Hindi by Sunita Jain

AMRUTLAL
– Udayan Thakker

With green ink, sometimes with red
Amrutlal would write down his poems
very carefully, in neat handwriting
in his leather-bound diary
Sometimes he had this terrible nightmare
that he died of the plague
that after his death his poems
were never published
not even found
But Amrutlal lived a long life
(He was my friend)
During his lifetime he saw
the birth of his "Collection of Poems"
He also saw it age
and die.

Amrutlal: Someone who is immortal

Translated from Gujarati by the poet.

AN ASIAN CHILD ENTERS A BRITISH CLASSROOM
– Debjani Chatterjee

Before she stepped into the classroom:
she removed coat, mittens and chunni;
mentally undid her shoes for entry
to a temple of secular mystery.

She also shed her:
language, name, identity;
donned the mask of neat conformity,
prepared for lessons in cultural anonymity.

English

AN INVITATION
– Vallana

Make haste, traveller, be on your way!
These woods are alive with beasts,
it's almost dusk, and you're awfully young
to be travelling on your own.
I can't invite you to stay here—
a young girl like me, home alone.

Transcreated from Sanskrit by Amanda Bell

AN ORANGE
– Jibanananda Das

Once I have left this body
Shall I not return to earth?
Let me come back
On a winter night
As the doleful flesh of a chilled orange
At the bedside of a dying friend

Translated from Bengali by Arunava Sinha

AND DEATH DEMANDS A LABOR

– Sumita Chakraborty

When it rains in Boston, from each street rises
the smell of sea. So do the faces of the dead.
For my father, I will someday write:
On this day endeth this man, who did all he could
to craft the most intricate fears, this man
whose waking dreams were of breaking the small bones
in the feet of all the world's birds. Father.
You know the stories. You were raised on them.
To end a world, a god dances. To kill a demon,
a goddess turns into one. Almanacs of annihilation
are chronicled in cosmic time. Go on.
Batter everything of mine that you can find.
Find my roe deer with the single antler. Kill him.
Find a girl, or a woman. Display to me her remains
on some unpaved expanse, like road kill
on Kentucky highways, turning from flesh to a
fine sand made of ground bone, under a sun
whose surface reaches temperatures six times hotter
than the finest crematory. On the surface of the earth,
our remains are in unholy concert with the remains
of all who have gone before and all who will follow,
and with all who live. In this way, our ground
resembles a bone house. Search in my body
for my heart, find it doesn't sit gently
where you learned it to be. Thieve in my armory.
Take my saws, take my torches, and drown
my phalanx of bees. Carve into me the words
of the chronicler of hell. Make your very best
catastrophe. My piano plays loud and fast
although my hands are nowhere to be found.
Father, as you well know, I am but a woman.
I believe in neither gods nor goddesses.

I have left my voice up and down the seam
of this country. I, unlike you, need no saws,
or torches. The bees you drowned will come to me
again. Each time you bear your weapons, I,
no more than a woman, grow a new limb.
Each time you use a weapon, my sinews grow
like vines that devour a maple tree.
When I cry, my face becomes the inescapable sea,
and when you drain blood from a creature,
I drink it. On this day this man died,
having always eaten the good food
amid the angry ghosts, having always made
the most overwrought hells.
On this day the moon waxes gibbous
and the moths breed in the old carpets.
On this day from a slit in the ground rises
a girl who does not live long.
On this day to me a lover turns his back
and will not meet my eye.
On this day the faces of the death-marked
are part-willow, part-lion.
On this day has died an artist of ugly tapestries,
and his wares burst into flame.
On this day endeth this man upon who
I hurl the harvest of this ghostly piano,
and on the surface of this exceptional world
the birds have all come to our thresholds,
our windows and our doors, our floorboards,
our attic crannies and underground storerooms,
wires and railroads, tarmacs, highways,
cliffs and oceans, and have all begun to laugh,
a sound like an orange and glittering fire
that originates from places unseen.

English

APPARITION ON THE RIVER BANK

– Bhojya Deva

She squeezes her dripping hair
and from that black lightning
a few sparkling drops trickle.
She stretches her arms up and examines
the firmness of her glistening breasts.
A wet, transparent skirt clings to her thighs.
Bending forward, she scans the bank
before emerging out of the river.

Transcreated from Sanskrit by Bill Wolak and Abhay K.

ASHTAVAKRA GITA CH-1

1: Instruction on Self Realization

Janaka said:

1.1 Master,
how is Knowledge to be achieved,
detachment acquired,
liberation attained?

Ashtavakra said:

1.2 To be free,
shun the experiences of the senses
like poison.
Turn your attention to
forgiveness, sincerity, kindness, simplicity, truth.

1.3 You are not earth, water, fire or air.
Nor are you empty space.
Liberation is to know yourself
as Awareness alone—
the Witness of these.

1.4 Abide in Awareness
with no illusion of person.
You will be instantly free and at peace.

1.5 You have no caste or duties.
You are invisible, unattached, formless.
You are the Witness of all things.
Be happy.

1.6 Right and wrong, pleasure and pain,
exist in mind only.
They are not your concern.

You neither do, nor enjoy.
You are free.

1.7 You are the Solitary Witness
of All That Is,
forever free.
Your only bondage is not seeing This.

1.8 The thought: 'I am the doer'
is the bite of a poisonous snake.
To know: 'I do nothing'
is the wisdom of faith.
Be happy.

1.9 A single understanding:
'I am the One Awareness,
consumes all suffering
in the fire of an instant.
Be happy.

1.10 You are unbounded Awareness—
Bliss, Supreme Bliss—
in which the universe appears
like the mirage of a snake in a rope.
Be happy.

1.11 It is true what they say:
'You are what you think.'
If you think you are bound you are bound.
If you think you are free you are free.

1.12 You are Self—the Solitary Witness.
You are perfect, all-pervading, One.
You are free, desireless, forever still.
The universe is but a seeming in You.

1.13 Meditate on this: 'I am Awareness alone—Unity itself.'
Give up the idea that you are separate, a person,
that there is within and without.

1.14 You have long been bound thinking:
'I am a person.'
Let the knowledge: 'I am Awareness alone'
be the sword that frees you.

1.15 You are now and forever
free, luminous, transparent, still.
The practice of meditation
keeps one in bondage.

1.16 You are pure Consciousness—
the substance of the universe.
The universe exists within you.
Don't be small-minded.

1.17 You are unconditioned, changeless, formless.
You are solid, unfathomable, cool.
Desire nothing.
You are Consciousness.

1.18 That which has form is not real.
Only the formless is permanent.
Once this is known,
you will not return to illusion.

1.19 Just as a mirror exists
both within and without
the image reflected,
the Supreme Self exists
both within and without the body.

1.20 Just as the same space exists
both within and without a jar,
the timeless, all-pervasive One
exists as Totality.

Translated from Sanskrit by Bart Marshall

AUBADE

– Jayshankar Prasad

Awake for the night is spent.
In the well of the sky the dawn
dips her vessel of stars
to the sound of birds at their morning-song.
The young leaves
are a veil, swaying.
How soft along the vine are the buds of Spring!

Awake for the night is spent.
Your lips hold life in a stillness;
your hair entraps the south-wind.
Ah, you are asleep with the night-song filling your eyes!
Awake. The night is spent.

Translated from Hindi by Romila Thapar

AUBADE
– R. Parthasarathy

You wake up and slip quietly out of the room,
shutting the door behind you. Eyes closed,
I clasp your pillow in hopes of smelling out
the faintest trace of your body's secret perfume.

Never before have I held you more closely
than I hold you now in your absence,
but you hug the morning paper to your chest
in the kitchen and wash it down with a cup of tea.

English

BARDIC STUFF
– Manohar Shetty

Poets are natural-born schizoids
And psychoanalysts
Have no answer to them.

On the surface they appear
As normal as toast and eggs
And mundane as salt.

But something odd is burning
Them up, something in the blood
That does not show up

In clinical tests or before a judicial
Bench or a bevy of angels,
Gods or painted devils.

All the accoutrements
Of riches and success don't
Seem much to them.

Though they nod and smile
Genially, their minds are a
Permanent someplace else.

One half of their world
Is streaked white and blue, the other
Scarred as the moon

Or to use a more earthly
Simile, they're like those
Camels with not one but

Two humps of water
To carry them through
The scorching dunes.

Traditionally their money,
If they have any,
Drains out like a hose pipe

Forgotten in a garden.
It seems endless, this business
Of planting a poem which

May die as a sapling before
They move on to the next
Though no one is listening

Just as no one does to starlings
Or nightingales, hooting owls,
The trumpeting blue whale

Or to the sound of the planet
Grinding slowly on
Its creaking axis.

English

BARS
– Keki N. Daruwalla

If you want
a cage, my dear
you do not have
to travel far.
If you want to feel
hemmed in,
you'll be hemmed in.
Look for scars
you'll be full of scars.
Even light can turn
into a cage.
The cage of light
has seven bars.

English

BEGGAR
– Angshuman Kar

Without informing us
sometimes our friends change their numbers
With whatever force we press the green button then
and dial the old number
it does not ring

Sometimes, however, it rings
and an unknown grave voice says
'wrong number'.

Sometimes
it rings and I hear 'hello'...
I think I am talking to my old friend
I keep on talking
ten seconds elapse, twenty seconds
the line does not get disconnected
then, after sometime,
the person who, in a slightly melancholic voice says
'wrong number'
is too a beggar of words
without informing him
his friends too
have changed their numbers!

Translated from Bengali by Dr Ajoy Ranjan Biswas

BIRTHPLACE WITH BURIED STONES

– Meena Alexander

I

In the absence of reliable ghosts I made aria,
Coughing into emptiness, and it came

A west wind from the plains with its arbitrary arsenal:
Torn sails from the Ganga river,

Bits of spurned silk,
Strips of jute to be fashioned into lines,

What words stake—sentence and make-believe,
A lyric summoning.

II

I came into this world in an Allahabad hospital,
Close to a smelly cow pasture.

I was brought to a barracks, with white walls
And corrugated tin roof,

Beside a civil aviation training center.
In World War II officers were docketed there.

I heard the twang of propellers,
Jets pumping hot whorls of air,

Heaven bent,
Blessing my first home.

III

In an open doorway, in half darkness
I see a young woman standing.

Her breasts are swollen with milk.
She is transfixed, staring at a man,

His hair gleaming with sweat,
Trousers rolled up

Stepping off his bicycle,
Mustard bloom catches in his shirt.

I do not know what she says to him,
Or he to her, all that is utterly beyond me.

Their infant once a clot of blood
Is spectral still.

Behind this family are vessels of brass
Dotted with saffron,

The trunk of a mango tree chopped into bits,
Ready to be burnt at the household fire.

IV

Through the portals of that larger chaos,
What we can scarcely conceive of in our minds—

We'd rather think of starry nights with biting flames
Trapped inside tree trunks, a wellspring of desire

Igniting men and gods,
A lava storm where butterflies dance—

Comes bloodletting at the borders,
Severed tongues, riots in the capital,

The unspeakable hurt of history:
So the river Ganga pours into the sea.

V

In aftermath—the elements of vocal awakening:
Crud, spittle, snot, menstrual blistering,

Also infant steps, a child's hunger, a woman's rage
At the entrance to a kitchen,

Her hands picking up vegetable shavings, chicken bones,
Gold tossed from an ancestral keep.

All this flows into me as mottled memory,
Mixed with syllables of sweat, gashed syntax,

Strands of burst bone in river sand,
Beside the buried stones of Sarasvati Koop—

Well of mystic sky-water where swans
Dip their throats and come out dreaming.

English

BLACK BAG
– Pavankumar Jain

I have a desire
To put an end to my life,
But not today,
There's nothing special
About today.

Moreover,
I have two glass bottles to clean,
A haircut to get,
My cataracts operated,
Plants to water
(They're flowering at the moment),
A younger sister to look after.
And I haven't stopped dreaming of the stranger
Who'll leave me his millions.

For now I'll put
The talk of death
In my tattered black shopping bag
Full of holes
And hang it from a nail
In the wall.

To be honest,
I'd like to become a sadhu.
But it'll be years before I can bring
Any sort of order to the chaos
That surrounds me.
There's also the awkwardness
Of moving around in a loincloth,
Begging for alms.
That's one thing.

Then, there are the mothers
Who'll want to scare their little ones
By pointing at us:
There goes a sadhu.
He's come to catch you.
It's not easy to get used to all this.

Best that I put this away too
In my tattered black shopping bag
Full of holes
And hang it from a nail
In the wall.

Translated from Gujarati by Arvind Krishna Mehrotra

BONE OF TIME
– Jayanta Mahapatra

Is this why one always remembers:
the autumn night struggling with its breath,
the fireflies pulsing and drawing back
to reveal the fallen teeth of the forest:
and the moon, to whom we owe
the tempests of light among the shadows,
seeking refuge
in a narrow window of our wakefulness.

The last time I saw you, I told myself:
I would see nothing, never again,
and the evening stars that fall to earth
could make the distance between us no shorter.
Your window looks so warm from here,
and the wind drifts away noiselessly
across the comfortless river: bone of time
that makes each one understand
how night is night; and through it
to enter the kingdom where Orion turns
calm and certain, into neither darkness nor light.

English

BREASTS

– Kutti Revathi

Breasts
are bubbles, rising from marshlands.

As they gently swelled and blossomed
at due season, at Time's edge,
I watched over them in amazement.

Never speaking to anyone else
they are with me always
singing
of quiet sorrow
of love
of ecstasy.

They have never forgotten
to enthuse the seed-beds
of all my changing seasons.

At times of penance
they struggle and strain;
and at the thrust and pull of lust
like the proud ascent of music
they stand erect.

From the press of an embrace
they distil love; from the shock
of childbirth
milk, flowing from blood.

Like two teardrops,
which cannot be wiped away
when love is thwarted,
they fill, and they overflow.

Translated from Tamil by Lakshmi Holmström

BREATH
– Lal Ded

I trapped my breath in the bellows of my throat:
a lamp blazed up inside, showed me who I really was.
I crossed the darkness holding fast to that lamp,
scattering its light-seeds around me as I went.

Translated from Kashmiri by Ranjit Hoskote

BUDDHA ON THE HIGHWAY
– Kalpatta Narayanan

Yesterday
I saw Buddha cross the road.
I had been waiting long on this side
unable to cross in the evening rush
thinking how we wait for a year
or a year and a half in order to cross the road
in a life fifty, sixty or seventy years long.

He crossed the road, slow, fearless.
As I began to follow him
a vehicle rushed forward screaming at me.

No vehicle slowed down for him;
he just walked along
a wild, wide, desolate path
which was always there
and reached the other side.

Translated from Malayalam by K. Satchidanandan

CHAMPA

– Katyayani

Champa grew up
among seven brothers

She was as flexible
as the bamboo reed
snakily she disturbed
her father's sleep
became the black shadow
of his dreams
Champa grew up
among seven brothers.

She was pounded
with the paddy
and thrown away
as garbage with the husk.
A parasitic creeper
grew at that spot.
Champa grew up
among seven thorny bushes.
She returned home once more.

Champa, who grew up
among seven brothers, was found
hanging from the roof
of the house.
She was buried in the web
of water hyacinths
a blue lotus appeared there.

Champa returned home once again
to be offered to the gods

when she wilted
she was crushed and burnt.
Her ashes were scattered
over the whole village.
It rained heavily at night
The next day
outside each door
among the wild *nagphani* weeds
alone and unafraid
Champa was seen smiling.

Nagphani: Cactus

Translated from Hindi by Nirupama Dutt

CHILL OUT

– Anon

Busy right now with my precious bamboo flute,
my delicate fingers on the holes.
Darling, can't snuggle you now,
I'm lost fiddling this melodious flute.
Chill out - eat some chilli!
Can't squeeze you right now.
Busy with my precious little bamboo flute,
my delicate fingers on the holes.

Transcreated from Gondi by Gabriel Rosenstock and Abhay K.

CITY OF MEMORIES

– Sunil Gangopadhyay

People at the borders speak prose
In ghettoes and factories they speak prose
During the day the city speaks prose
All contemporary miseries speak prose
The parched field and the rough unkempt men speak prose
The entire civilization of scissors and knives talk prose.
What then shall poetry be about?

Translated from Bengali by Kalyan Roy and Bonnie MacDougall

CONSISTENTLY IGNORED
– G.S. Sharat Chandra

Consistently ignored in a family of ten
I asked mother, 'Am I your real son?'
She paused from grinding spice,
'No, I bought you from a beggar
For a bushel of rice!'
From behind, sisters giggled.

I matched features, spied on beggars,
Roamed the backyard thinking
Of distant huts, certain
My mother sat busy in one
Scheming to trade another son
For fish to add to that bushel.

English

CONVERSATION PIECE
– Eunice de Souza

My Portuguese-bred colleague
picked up a clay *shivalingam*
one day and said:
Is this an ashtray?
No, said the salesman.
This is our god.

Shivalingam: The phallus of Lord Shiva worshipped by the Hindus

English

DANCE OF SHIVA
– Hoshang Merchant

By my bed Shiva dances
his left leg over his head
his hair, fire, sacred thread, anklet flying

In my bed
he and I have become a pillar
kneeling at prayer

Difficult to separate god from supplicant
we have flowed into each other
meanwhile the Lord has danced his own round

Making poor, rich
The ancient, young again
And night, day
Cloud, rain

English

DARING

– Padma Sachdev

No one drinks from the well
to the right of our hill,
though it brims with bright water;
no one glances that way,
since a calf drowned in its depths,
deceived by drifting blossoms.
Deep in its core, shadows yearn
for their return—the girls with vessels.
The water calls to me in daylight,
implores me to imbibe it
in full sight. At night, I bathe
unseen in its darkness, cup
its coolness in my palms
and raise it to my mouth—
my thirst is as insatiable as love.

Transcreated from Dogri by Amanda Bell

DAWN IN WINTER
– Agyeya

Just enough light
for darkness to show
Just enough rain
for silence to sound
Just enough pain to remember
that I have forgotten
I have forgotten...

Translated from Hindi by Lucy Rosenstein

DAY AFTER DAY

– Annamaya

Life, day after day, is a game
To find what you cannot see
    is truth.
Coming is real. Going is real.
What you do in between is a game.
Right in front of you
lies the world.
At the very end
is truth.
We eat food. We wear clothes.
It's all part of this passing game.
The past clings to our bodies.
Cross the doorway:
there is truth.
Badness never ends,
and there's never enough good.
In the end, time is a game.
High on the mountain, God is king.
Higher than heaven
is truth.

Translated from Telugu by Velcheru Narayana Rao and David Shulman

DEATH OF A ROGUE ELEPHANT
– N. N. Kakkad

As the last trumpeting of the rogue
elephant was heard over the foundations
of unfinished houses, he said to himself:

Is the forest far or near?
The darkness and solitude of the dense
forest stains the evening,
but, scattered all around is
the sprawling, unfinished metropolis.

Streets are empty,
infinitely broad, infinitely long
always criss-crossing
only foundations of houses
a row stretching to infinity
somewhere the remembrance of the sea.

The last trumpeting of the rogue
elephant hit by the bullet
slowly dissolved into silence
The blackness of the dusk
sucked that grief dry
along with the evening sky's blood.

I alone…
I alone walk
not knowing why
along the unfinished walls of these houses.

Translated from Malayalam by E.V. Ramakrishnan

DECEPTION

– Sampurna Chattarji

everything seems to glide and dance
in synchronicity the trains come and go sliding
past each other
the motor boats appear at the same spot
the birds sink towards the tracks
the light moves
people walk into the light
the most secret god is a clock

English

DESCRIPTION OF THE MISSING ONE
– Kunwar Narain

Wheatish-complexion, rustic ways,
    on his brow the scar of a wound,
height not under five feet,
    talks as if he has never known grief.

Stutters.
His age? Somewhat more than many thousands of years, he says.
Looks a bit crazed – but isn't.
Has often fallen off heights and got all broken up

Hence, when seen, will look pieced together
like the map of India.

Translated from Hindi by Apurva Narain

DIGAMBARA
– Anitha Thampi

A lone bowstring
I stretch taut
above the endless earth.

Taking in his two hands
this sky's bow
strung tight,
raising it
like time
touching life
possessed by dreams,
with fear,
with intense love,
he holds the bow
targeting infinity
and shoots into the night
millions of stars.

Digambara: Someone whose garment is the sky. It is also a sect of Jainism.

Translated from Malayalam by K. Satchidanandan

DO NOT ASK
– H.S. Shivaprakash

Do not ask me who brought water
Into the blazing midday's silence
Do not ask who brought me light
Into my prison in netherworlds

Do not ask who brought cooling breeze
To the pyre-ridden cremation ground
Do not ask me who brought a poem
To the market's din and bustle

Do not ask me who brought the spring
To my land wrecked with famines
Do not say: Shiva Prakash. Not me,
But it is you, you and you alone

Translated from Kannada by the poet

DOTHEAD

– Amit Majmudar

Well yes, I said, my mother wears a dot.
I know they said 'third eye' in class, but it's not
an *eye* eye, not like that. It's not some freak
third eye that opens on your forehead like
on some Chernobyl baby. What it means
is, what it's *showing* is, there's this unseen
eye, on the inside. And she's marking it.
It's how the X that says where treasure's at
is not the treasure, but as good as treasure.—
All right. What I said wasn't half so measured.
In fact, I didn't say a thing. Their laughter
had made my mouth go dry. Lunch was after
World History; that week was India—myths,
caste system, suttee, all the Greatest Hits.
The white kids I was sitting with were friends,
at least as I defined a friend back then.
So wait, said Nick, does *your* mom wear a dot?
I nodded, and I caught a smirk on Todd—
She wear it to the shower? And to bed?—
while Jesse sucked his chocolate milk and Brad
was getting ready for another stab.
I said, Hand me that ketchup packet there.
And Nick said, What? I snatched it, twitched the tear,
and squeezed a dollop on my thumb and worked
circles till the red planet entered the house of war
and on my forehead for the world to see
my third eye burned those schoolboys in their seats,
their flesh in little puddles underneath,
pale pools where Nataraja cooled his feet.

English

EASY, FRIEND
– Kabir

Easy, friend.
What's the big fuss about?

Once dead,
The body that was stuffed with
Kilos of sweets
Is carried out to be burnt,
And the head on which
A bright turban was tied
Is rolled by crows in the dust.
A man with a stick
Will poke the cold ashes
For your bones.

But I'm wasting my time,
Says Kabir.
Even death's bludgeon
About to crush your head
Won't wake you up.

Translated from Hindi by Arvind Krishna Mehrotra

ENGRAVING OF A BISON ON STONE

– Arvind Krishna Mehrotra

The land resists
Because it cannot be
Tempted, or broken
In a chamber. It records,
By carefully shuffling the leaves,
The passage of each storm, rain,
And drought. The land yields
In places, deliberately,
Having learnt warfare from the armies
It fed. The land is of one
Piece and hasn't forgotten
Old miracles: the engraving of a bison
On stone, for instance. The land
Turns up like an unexpected
Visitor and gives refuge, it cannot be
Locked or put away. The land
Cannot sign its name, it cannot die
Because it cannot be buried,
It understands the language,
It speaks in dialect.

English

EPITAPH
– Mohammad Alvi

As soon as I reached the grave
I stretched my limbs to rest
thinking no one would disturb me now,
these two yards of land are mine alone
and so I kept turning into soil
losing count of time
but soon my peace was disturbed
somebody else entered my grave
and his epitaph
is carved on my stone.

Translated from Urdu by Anisur Rahman

EPITAPH

– Shakti Chattopadhyay

He gave up none of the world's pleasures;
He was a poet and a scrounge.

Rejoice! said his publishers. The fellow's dead.
At least he won't now turn up threateningly at the office,
Dressed for the evening, demanding his royalties:
The money, you swine, or I'll gut the place.

And so he was laid on the pyre – poet, troublemaker, pauper.

Translated from Bangla by Arvind Krishna Mehrotra

EPITAPH ON MY GRAVESTONE
– Manushya Puthiran

There is
no one here.
You may go.

Translated from Tamil by C.S. Lakshmi and Arundhati Subramaniam

EVERY LAND OUR HOME
– Kaniyan Punkunran

Every land is our home, and every man is one of us.
Good and evil don't flow from others.
Pain and help for pain appear by themselves.
Even death isn't new. We don't rejoice
that life is sweet, nor are we laid waste by grief.
Like a raft swirling in the waters of a deep river
that roars and crashes upon the rocks
in a thunderstorm under skies bruised by lightning,
our life, dear as it is, takes its usual course.
Wise men, who foresee all things, know this.
And so we don't stand in awe of the great,
much less do we hold the small in contempt.

Translated from Tamil by R. Parthasarathy

EXILE

– Ravi Shankar

There's nowhere else I'd rather not be than here,
But here I am, nonetheless, dispossessed,
Though not quite, because I never owned
What's been taken from me, never have belonged
In and to a place, a people, a common history.
Even as a child when I was slurred in school -
Towel head, dot boy, camel jockey -
None of the abuse was precise: only Sikhs
Wear turbans, widows and young girls bindis,
Not one species of camel is indigenous to India . . .
If, as Simone Weil writes, to be rooted
Is the most important and least recognized need
Of the human soul, behold: I am an epiphyte.
I conjure sustenance from thin air and the smell
Of both camphor and meatloaf equally repel me.
I've worn a lungi pulled between my legs,
Done designer drugs while subwoofers throbbed,
Sipped masala chai steaming from a tin cup,
Driven a Dodge across the Verrazano in rush hour,
And always to some degree felt extraneous,
Like a meteorite happened upon bingo night.
This alien feeling, honed in aloneness to an edge,
Uses me to carve an appropriate mask each morning.
I'm still unsure what effect it has on my soul.

English

EYES
– Vasant Abaji Dahake

A night like opium
when the moonlight moans through the water,
that's how your eyes

brim over my face.

Translated from Marathi by Ranjit Hoskote

FAMINE AND AFTER

– Nagarjuna

For days and days the hearth stayed cold, the hand mill quiet
For days and days the one-eyed bitch slept nearby
For days and days lizards paced on the wall
For days and days rats too were miserable

Grain came to the house after many a day
Smoke rose above the courtyard after many a day
The eyes of the household shone after many a day
The crow scratched its feathers after many a day.

Translated from Hindi by Nalini Taneja

FAREWELL
– Jiban Narah

On the day our sister departed
she left an unbearable emptiness in her wake.
Because she loved to sing alone
a room of her own was built.
The sad resonance of her singing
scattered in the room—
it hurts us still from time to time.
She left us forever
with the boy she loved—that's the custom,
not easy to accept.
Because she loved the *simalu* blossom
she never told a lie to the river.
The day she sailed downstream
her sorrow began to grow.

Simalu: Silk-cotton tree

Translated from Assamese by Lyra Neog

FATHER RETURNING HOME
– Dilip Chitre

My father travels on the late evening train
standing among silent commuters
Suburbs slide past his unseeing eyes
His shirt and pants are soggy and his black raincoat
stained with mud and his bag stuffed with books
is falling apart. His eyes dimmed by age
fade homeward through the humid monsoon night
Now I can see him getting off the train
like a word dropped from a long sentence
He hurries across the length of the grey platform,
crosses the railway line, enters the lane
His *chappals* are sticky with mud but he hurries onwards
Home again, I see him drinking weak tea,
eating a stale *chapati*, reading a book.
He goes into the toilet to contemplate
man's estrangement from a man-made world
Coming out he trembles at the sink,
the cold water running over his brown hands,
a few drops cling to the greying hair on his wrists
His sullen children have often refused to share
jokes and secrets with him. He will now go to sleep
listening to the static on the radio, dreaming
of his ancestors and grandchildren, thinking
of nomads entering a subcontinent through a narrow pass.

Chappals: Slippers
Chapati: Indian bread

Translated from Marathi by the poet

FOREST BALLADS

– Niranjan Chakma

After each devastating storm
a silence descends on the entire hill.
Distraught birds are puzzled!
Should they return to their shattered nests
or go out in search of food?
One fine morning the birds are afflicted
with an identity crisis.
The name currently used to spot them
had never been heard by them before.

Recently a huge debate about their identity and rights
rocked a scholarly Geneva conference.
References were copiously made to the Vedas.
Stale, century-old theories of the expansionists
were presented with great gusts.
But these participants
had never tried to understand
the forest ballads.

Translated from Chakma by Udayan Ghosh

FOUR HAIKU AND A TANKA
– K. Ramesh

abandoned dog ...
looking at the face of
every pedestrian

—

power failure…
closing the book
I listen to the rain

—

pause in the traffic
small yellow leaves
cross the road

—

a village in the mountains
a stray dog becomes
our trek guide

—

summer twilight –
a girl steps out
of the house where
birds keep chirping
in a cage

English

FRIEND, THIS IS THE ONLY WAY
– Sachal Sarmast

Friend, this is the only way
to learn the secret way:

Ignore the paths of others,
even the saints' steep trails.

Don't follow.
Don't journey at all.

Rip the veil from your face.

Translated from Sindhi by Ivan M. Granger

FROGS
– Buddhadev Bose

Monsoon rains pour down, and the frogs get delirious
singing like a chorus with loud elated voices.
Today there's nothing to fear: neither drought,
nor shortage of warmth,
neither snake's jaws, nor rocks thrown by mischievous boys.
As the grasses thicken like green clouds,
in the bountiful flooded fields
their fleeting splash of immortality echoes louder and louder with
every leap.
They have no necks, but their throats bulge and resonate,
and what smooth bodies, what eyes like cold gemstones—
eyes gazing upwards, unwavering in meditation,
ecstatic, lidless, like the eyes of holy men fixed on God.
The rain comes to an end; the shadows tilt.
Their songs drift like hymns in the expectant air.
Now daylight vanishes silently, but a solemn murmur
stings the twilight, and the translucent sky bends down to hear.
Night and rain, and we're cozy in bed.
Only a single incessant melody resonates through our sleep
like the final lines of a mystic incantation—
the last frog's frenetic croaking, croaking, croaking.

Transcreated from Bengali by Bill Wolak

GIANT BUILDINGS
– Munibur Rahman

All our lives
we have crawled into the shadow
of giant buildings,
clinging onto the walls.

Buildings were towering peaks
and we were ants
always on the lookout for food.

Skyscrapers loomed in the way
whenever friends came together.

Those buildings grew taller
as we shrank.

At last, one day, we disappeared,
and left nothing behind
but giant buildings.

Transcreated from Urdu by Gabriel Rosenstock and Abhay K.

GIRLS ON ROOFTOPS
– Alok Dhanwa

Still the girls come on to the rooftops
Their shadows fall on my life

The girls are here for the boys
Downstairs, amidst bullets, the boys play cards
Sitting, on the stairs above the drain
Lazing on benches outside the footpath tea-stall
Sipping tea
Around a boy who plays the mouth-organ sweet
Timeless tunes of *Awara, Sree 420.*

A *newspaperwallah* spreads his wares
And some young men read the early edition
Not all are students
Some unemployed yet, small timers some
Whilers, lumpens

But in their veins, bloodstreams
They await a girl
A hope—that from these houses and rooftops
One day, some day—love will arrive.

Awara, Sree 420: popular Hindi films
Newspaperwallah: Someone who delivers newspapers door to door

Translated from Hindi by the poet

GOD

– Anuradha Mahapatra

I've never seen God, but when I notice temples,
I think of Hiranyakashypu, the demon king,
and when I watch a statue worshipped
I think about someone's daughter
being sold for cash. One vanishing life offered to another.
But to see blood coughed from the mouths of the bloodless
is the ultimate joke.

Still, when I spotted that guy
in the filthy blue t-shirt on the train,
stiff as a cast-iron cannon, I wished he were God!
Then at least I could have found a safe hiding place,
or I could have attacked him,
but even if I'd murdered him,
it would have been an act of love.
Nowadays, even when I step onto the bus
I'm thinking about God.

Transcreated from Bengali by Bill Wolak

GRANDFATHER'S PHOTOGRAPH
– Mangalesh Dabral

Grandfather wasn't fond of being photographed
or didn't find the time perhaps
There's just one picture of him
hanging on an old discolored wall
He looks serious and composed
like a cloud heavy with water
All we know of Grandfather is
that he gave alms to beggars
tossed restlessly in his sleep
and made his bed neatly every morning
I was just a kid then
and never noticed his anger or
his ordinariness
Pictures never show your helpless side
Mother used to tell us that
when we fell asleep surrounded
by strange creatures of the night
Grandfather would stay awake inside the picture
I didn't grow as tall as Grandfather
nor as composed or as serious
Still something in me resembles him
An anger like his
an ordinariness
I too walk with my head lowered
and every day see myself
sitting in an empty
picture frame.

Translated from Hindi by Arvind Krishna Mehrotra

HE IS A POET
– Shankar Ramani

He is a poet, solitary and lonely.
Through the window of his ramshackle house
he watches the sky, day and night.
He is completely crazy
Don't call him closer
Nor talk to him;
Don't even look at him;
You never know
when he would throw
on your body
a basketful of pebbles
But if and when his window
turns into the blue sky
the birds from across the horizon
beckon him to the ethereal light.

Translated from Konkani by Damodar Mauzo

HE PROMISED HE'D RETURN TOMORROW
– Vidyapati

He promised he'd return tomorrow.
And I wrote everywhere on my floor:
"Tomorrow."

The morning broke, when they all asked:
Now tell us, when will your "Tomorrow" come?
Tomorrow, Tomorrow, where are you?
I cried and cried, but my Tomorrow never returned!

Vidyapati says: O listen, dear!
Your Tomorrow became a today
with other women.

Translated from Maithali by Azfar Hussain

HERE COMES GOD

– Tenetti Suri

Hey, here comes god,
lifeless in bronze,
parading the streets,
riding his wooden horse.

Ask him about wages, fellows.
Tell him we don't have
enough to eat.

The wise men tell us
even stone hearts melt.
Let's see if that's true.

Bow down to him,
see if he listens,
and let go if he doesn't answer.

Hold up your hands
millions at once
raise your voice
so the sky itself shivers.

Ask him about the wages, fellows.
Tell him we don't have
enough to eat.

Translated from Telugu by Velcheru Narayan Rao

HISTORY OF JUSTICE
– Rohan Chhetri

Some kids from the neighbourhood are bursting firecrackers
by the side of our compound wall. Grandmother is
screaming at them. Mother smiles knowing
they won't listen. Grandfather once stayed up
late in the night at the window of the first floor
waiting for the drunk who pissed on our wall
every night, so he could slosh a good whole bucket
of cold water over his head in the frosty winter night.
He's been dead since long, our grandfather.
But grandmother hasn't forgotten the battered face
of the man who was tied to a post outside the house
for having beaten his wife to a pulp. And grandfather
lunging his fists on the poor man's face. Grandmother
by the window thinking if she had married a monster.
Most of all, the face of her young husband during the time
of the revolution when she went to see him in the lockup,
where he was hung naked upside down for two days,
with mud shoved in his mouth by the Bengali Inspector who
kept saying, *Feed him the land, that's what they are fighting for*

English

HORSE PLAY

– K. Ayyappa Paniker

Four gallant horses
galloped forth.
One was white, one was black,
one was red, one was brown.
One had four legs,
the other had three,
the third horse had two,
and the fourth one had only one.
The one-legged horse
said to the others:
the time for dance has come
dear friends,
let's dance on a single hoof.
All of them were in a thrall
and the dance began.
The four-legged horse fainted instantly,
the three-legged slipped and fell,
the two-legged limped and crashed
only the one-legged horse
danced on and on.

Translated from Malayalam by K. Satchidanandan

HOW CAN A RIVER REJECT ITS FISH? – Janabai

If the Ganga empties into the sea
and the sea abandons her,
tell me, Vitthal, who would
hear her complaint?

How can a river reject its fish?
How can a mother desert her child?
Jana says, Lord,
accept those who surrender.

Transcreated from Marathi by Bill Wolak

HOW TO GO TO THE TAO TEMPLE
– K. Satchidanandan

Don't lock the door.
Go lightly like the leaf in the breeze
along the dawn's valley.
If you are too fair,
cover yourself with ash.
If too clever, go half-asleep.
That which is fast
will tire fast:
be slow, slow as stillness.

Be formless like water.
Lie low, don't even try to go up.
Don't go round the deity:
nothingness has no directions,
no front, no back.
Don't call it by name,
its name has no name.
No offerings: empty pots
are easier to carry than full ones.
No prayers too: desires
have no place here.

Speak silently, if speak you must:
like the rock speaking to the trees
and leaves to flowers.
Silence is the sweetest of voices
and Nothingness has
the fairest of colours.
Let none see you coming
and none, going.
Cross the threshold shrunken
like one crossing a river in winter.

You have only a moment here
like the melting snow.

No pride: you are not even formed.
No anger: not even dust
is at your command.
No sorrow: it doesn't alter anything.
Renounce greatness:
there is no other way to be great.
Don't ever use your hands:
They are contemplating
not love, but violence.
Let the fish lie in its water
and the fruit, on its bough.
The soft one shall survive the hard,
like the tongue that survives teeth.
Only the one who does nothing
can do everything.

Go, the unmade idol
awaits you.

Translated from Malayalam by the poet

HOW TO READ A BOOK
– Muddupalani

When you are reading, and you come to a thorn,
pull it out. Use your knowledge
to heal the book. Don't meddle with poets
who make a living out of finding fault.
They're bad news.

Translated from Telugu by Velcheru Narayana Rao and David Shulman

HOW TO TAME A PAIR OF NEW CHAPPALS

– Gopal Honnalgere

don't keep them together
don't allow them to talk to each other
they may form a trade union

don't leave them anytime near
a wall clock, law books, calendar, national flag
gandhi's portrait or newspaper
they may come to know about
independence day, satyagraha,
holidays, working hours, minimum wages and corruption

don't take them to your temple
they may at once come to know you are weak
your god is false and start biting you

don't take them anytime close to your dining table
they may ask for food
or cast their evil eyes on your sumptuous dinner
first use them only for short walks
then gradually increase the distance
they should never know the amount of work they have to do

pull their tight straps loose
let them feel happy
they are growing bigger
smear some old oil on the rough straps
let them feel they are anointed

now they are good subdued labourers
ready to work overtime
for your fat feet

Satyagraha: Exhortation for truth
Chappals: Slippers

English

I HAVE BROUGHT THE SACRIFICIAL GOAT

– Joy Goswami

Place the greens below the mound
I have brought the sacrificial animal, a goat

He has forgotten his previous beheading
Yet the mark remains
    Garland-like round his throat

Translated from Bengali by Sampurna Chattarji

I HAVE GIVEN BIRTH TO A SON
– Anonymous Bhil mother

Dear sweet sparrow, deliver this message for me:
Tell my father that I have given birth to a son
Tell my mother that I have given birth to a son
Ask my father to give me a new sari
Ask my mother for a multi-colour blouse
Tell my brother that I have a son
Ask him to give me a sari too
Tell my uncle that I have given birth to a son
Ask him to bring me a multi-colour blouse

Sari: A garment worn by Indian women

Translated from Bhili by Abraham Thuruthumalil

I WEAR MY WORDLESSNESS

– K. Srilata

I wear my wordlessness
like a tattered dress,
its stitches undone.
Twice a week,
I wash myself,
dress and all,
in a river of drowning words
in whose lungs,
the despair of poets
has long since settled.
And yet,
this!
a new-born fawn of a poem
taking its first steps.

English

ICE CUBES, CAKE & ROTI
– Souvik Bandopadhyay

On the first peg, Camus, Kafka, Sartre and Foucault
on the second peg, Dante, Neruda, Ginsberg and Picasso
on the third, Freud, Marx, Mayakovsky and Daniken—
    mixing them with ice cubes,
    sipping luxuriously,
    not noticing,
    when had the clock struck midnight.

But we had noted,
that, in his house, he has two dogs,
two servants, and a full moon,
and the dogs eat cake,
while, the servants, burnt *roti*.

Roti: Bread

Translated from Bengali by Neelav Bose

IMAGINARY NUMBER

– Vijay Seshadri

The mountain that remains when the universe is destroyed
is not big and is not small.
Big and small are

comparative categories, and to what
could the mountain that remains when the universe is destroyed
be compared?

Consciousness observes and is appeased.
The soul scrambles across the screes.
The soul,

like the square root of minus 1,
is an impossibility that has its uses.

English

IN HER LOVEMAKING SHE GRIEVES
– Gagan Gill

In her lovemaking, she grieves
In her grief, she makes love

In her lovemaking, she gives him a name
The one she gives the name is illusion
Maya, whose desire moves through her sleep

She knows, in the end
whatever name she calls him by
each name will only be an empty space.

Making love, she thinks
she is safe in her oblivion
in her longing, in her selfishness
She doesn't remember that
the one she desires
is just one fistful of bones.
Bones that come out of the crematorium
in just five minutes

Making love, she breathes
in his flesh, his marrow, his soul

Somewhere around here was his soul
Would she find it
in these fistful of bones?

Each time in her fear
she holds him tightly to her
Each time he slips out from her arms

in her lovemaking
in her grief

Translated from Hindi by J.P. Das, Arlene Zide and Madhu B. Joshi

IN THE DUST FOREVER

– Tarannum Riyaz

The winds will dance through the trees
Birds will sing to the gardens
Water will flow into the rivers
Dew drops will fall onto the grass
Evening orange will dissolve the peaks
Boys will play, run through the fields
Juliets will meet their Romeos
Mothers will sing to their children, lullabies
A fistful of ashes of my existence
Will be lost in the dust forever.

Translated from Urdu by Miraan Punjabi

IN THE EVENT OF CHANGE
– Tsering Wangmo Dhompa

I am saying primroses lined the pathway of toothless hedges.

I am saying the ocean shimmered like corrugated steel in the morning sun.

The context of my story changes when you enter. Then I am dung on the wall of the nomad's field. Then the everyday waking person.

I am nodding in your direction like fissures between dandelion fur. Seeing in your manner.

I am speaking your pace. Slippage of silk slippers.

I say you are losing sight. I say your breasts are dry shells.

I am afraid of what I am capable of doing.

This is all a manner of stating how I prepare myself to be loved.

English

INCURABLE

– Yaquin

I desire the door-sill of my beloved
    More than a king's house;
I desire the shadow of the wall where her beauty hides
    More than the Delhi palaces.
Why did you wait till spring;
Were not my hands already full of red-thorned roses?
    My heart is yours,
So that I know not which heart I hear sighing:
    Yaquin, Yaquin, Yaquin, foolish Yaquin.

Translated from Urdu by Edward Powys Mathers

JAISALMER – IV
– Gulammohamed Sheikh

The sun's twelve faces
blazed
and setting
froze
all the twelve worlds.
The orphaned sand just lay there,
and the clouds ran away, seeing their chance.
The stars grinned, impotent
when
all those houses on the desert's
edge
got up and left,
dead camels on their backs;
bundles and belongings
fell useless in the sand,
the riders' turbans flew in
shreds
like the feathers of birds
quite killed and eaten,
and
half-naked men
kept gulping
the desert's thorny air,
their mouths wide open.

Translated from Gujarati by the author and Adil Jussawalla

KABARIWALA
– Kavita A. Jindal

Upper Ridge Road, Delhi, 1975

At the door of our second-floor flat he sits on his haunches,
takes out his scales, weighs the bundles of newspapers,
talks more than usual as he places the kilo and half-kilo weights;
he makes my mother suspicious at his chirpiness.

She insists he weighs the papers again; they haggle
over the price he'll pay for seven kilos, how many paise
for each brown glass bottle, how much for each tin can;
and it's only when he hands over some rupees that he says

Next month my cousin or my uncle will come to collect
instead of me; I'm going away.
Going where, we ask; going foreign, he says.
I'm going where there is free love

Where you can be with whomever you want whenever
you want; probably England, that's where I'm going.
Will you be a kabariwala there, I ask.
Don't think so, he replies, packing away his scales.

Onto his young shoulders he hefts the sacks of papers, bottles
and cast-off pans, informing me that in foreign
they don't re-process old things.
He goes down the stairs whistling.

Kabariwala: A scrap dealer or a rag picker

English

KALLI

– Ajmer Rode

Kalli followed me 8 miles
to the market where cattle were traded
or sold like slaves.
Cows goats bullocks camels . . .

Kalli was black beautiful and six
the prime age for a water buffalo.
She was dry. Repelled bulls as if she had
decided not to get pregnant again.

Hard to afford, my father decided
to sell her. Kalli seemed to understand.
She obeyed as I led her
by the steel chain, one end in my hand

the other around her neck.
I was fifteen. Her nervousness was over
soon after we entered the market
where sellers occupied

their given spaces like matrimonials
on a large weekly page.
Kalli sat with no emotion on her face
like an ascetic close to nirvana.

I sat stood walked around like a
neglected calf. No body bought Kalli.
She followed me 8 miles back home
with no questions in her eyes.

I wasn't sure if my father was sad
or glad to see Kalli back. He just
looked at her like a family member
who had missed the train.

Translated from Punjabi by the poet

LAMINATION

– Shefali Debbarma

The Scheduled Tribe certificate
was issued under the seal and signature
of the Sub-Divisional Officer
in the year I was born.
Lest the valuable paper gets soiled
mother kept it safe
in the folds of her favourite garments
within the cane basket.
After a hundred years, today
her favourite garments have worn out,
turned into shreds
white ants have eaten up the cane basket.
Only the Scheduled Tribe certificate still shines
laminated and framed.

Translated from Kokborok by Saroj Chaudhuri

LET LOOSE THE STINGING BEES
– Kanji Patel

High the hills and high the *mahua* trees
O Birsa's folk

From the *mahuas* rises the sound of the leading *dhol*
Awaken your sleeping *nagadas*
O Birsa's folk
Gather all the Bhils of the hills
Range together the Bhils of the hills
O Birsa's folk
Do a count of the Bhils
O Birsa's folk
Twelve crores and thirty two lakhs
Count the years
O Birsa's folk
A lakh of moons and a crore of suns

The bullets rain from all directions
O Birsa's folk
The cannon balls *angrezi*, *desi*
Surrounded, in the hills and rivers
O Birsa's folk
Leave the *dhols*, pick up your bows
Surrounded, in the forests and rocks
O Birsa's folk

From the earthen pots
let loose the captured stinging bees

This song is based on a song of the Bhils in the Panchmahals, Gujarat.

The *Mahua* tree (Bassia latifolia or Madhuca latifolia) is considered sacred by the Bhils.

Birsa refers to Birsa Munda, a tribal hero and important figure in the Indian freedom struggle, leading the tribals of the Chhotanupur region into the struggle. His struggle was not only against the British but an emancipatory struggle of the tribal people against the Zamindars and money lenders exploiting them.

Dhol is a kind of drum.

Nagada is a drum played to announce the beginning of battle.

Translated from Gujarati by Gopika Jadeja

LINEAGE
– Attoor Raviverma

Granddad loved
the Union Jack
with its stripes and squares:
he was a village officer.

Dad hoisted a tricolor.
He was a freedom fighter.

I hold aloft a red flag.

My grandson's hands
hold a Yankee flag
with fifty stars.

Translated from Malayalam by K. Satchidanandan

LOVE IS EVERYDAY NEW AND FRESH

– Bulleh Shah

The day I learnt the lesson of love
I was scared of the mosque.
I looked around and entered a temple
Where many a drum was beaten.
Love is everyday new and fresh.

Tired of reading the Vedas and the Quran,
Kneeling and protesting, my forehead was rubbed off.
God is neither in the Hindu shrine nor at Mecca.
He who has found Him, he is enlightened.
Love is everyday new and fresh.

Burn the prayer mat, break the water pot,
Quit the rosary, throw the staff.
Lovers say at the top of their voice;
'Leave Kosher meat and eat the dead.'
Love is everyday new and fresh.

Heer and Ranjha have already met;
In vain, she looks for him in the orchard.
Ranjha lies in the folds of her arms.
Lost her senses, she has gained them back.
Love is everyday new and fresh.

Translated from Punjabi by K.S. Duggal

LOVE SONG
– Nirala

I'm a Brahmin's son
But have fallen
  for this girl.

A potter's daughter
We've hired to fetch water,
She comes every morning at the crack of dawn.
She's the one I'm after.

Black as a koel,
No curves to her figure,
Of marriageable age
But not yet married.
That's what did it,
  and a sigh escaped me.

Her loud knock on the door
Wakes up the house.
No one else knows what's going on.
She takes the water-pot,
The big one, and steps out again,
My eyes following her.
  I haven't lost heart.

February 22, 1939

Translated from Hindi by Arvind Krishna Mehrotra

MAGADH

– Srikant Verma

Which way lies the city of Magadh?
Listen, O rider of the horse.
From Magadh I come
And to Magadh
I must return.

Which way shall I turn?
To the North of South?
Or to the East of West?
Lo, there lies Magadh!
And now it is gone!

It was only yesterday
That I had left Magadh behind,
It was only yesterday
That the people of Magadh had said.
Do not leave Magadh
I had given them my word.
That before the Sun rises
I shall be back

And now there is no Magadh.

Aren't you looking for Magadh as well?
Brothers.
This is not the Magadh.
That you have read about in books
This is the Magadh which you
Like me
Have lost forever.

Magadh: An ancient Indian kingdom in southern Bihar where great Maurya and Gupta empires originated and Buddhism and Jainism developed.

Translated from Hindi by Mrinal Pande

MAKING A CHAIR
– Dileep Jhaveri

Making a chair is the most natural thing
and very easy

You can wait for autumn
for every leaf to fall
or you can pluck out leaves one by one
like a crow picking on mouse flesh
Pull down the tree like an elephant uprooting forests
and remove the twigs like a wolf tearing at the tendons
Split it apart like a crocodile the bones
Bore in holes like a woodpecker
Fixing staves in crosses and hammering nails is an ancient art
Make smooth the surface with putty provided by the pulp
Obtain paints from the ancestors of the trees
buried for billions of years to re-emerge through oil wells
Resins from the freshly peeled bark will provide the sheen

Now sit back on the chair set in veranda
and contemplate over the sprouting green of a grass blade
from a crack in the asphalted pavement
Patiently awaiting a forest

Translated from Gujarati by the poet

MAKING LOVE TO HER
– Dharmakirti

Making love to her lasts only moments
like a dream, illusion, ending in regret
I reflect upon this truth a hundred times
Yet my heart can't forget the gazelle-eyed girl.

Translated from Sanskrit by Abhay K.

MARRIED LOVE
– Srinivas Rayaprol

Every evening
I am met at the gate by my wife
her hair in disorder and her dress a mess
from the kitchen
and the girls hang on leaves of the gate
while my ancient car rolls in.
One carries my bag, the other
my lunch basket.
The day's work is over and I am home.
I have forgotten them all day and now
suddenly remember that I must
disappoint them again
for my evening is planned
for a meaningless excursion to the bars.
And the coffee which my wife has served
is cold in my mouth
and the tales the children have brought from school
are dull on my ears.
In spite of my love for them
I must disappoint them again tonight.

English

MEDITATIONS ON DESIRE
– Saleem Peeradina

1
I can never say
what I feel about you.
Listen hard
for syllables unspoken,
not yet formed.
As for words
that do surface,
frisk them thoroughly
before inviting them in.

3
Only in the abstract
can words attain
such luminosity.
On contact
with the flesh
they burn up.

9
This love
I send up
like a kite
gives the empty sky
something
to hold on to.

English

MOMENT
– Kaifi Azami

Life is the name given to a few moments, and
In but one of those fleeting moments
Two eyes meet eloquently
Looking up from a cup of tea, and
Enter the heart piercingly
And say,
Today do not speak
I'll be silent too
Let's just sit thus
Holding each other's hand
United by this gift of sorrow
Bonded by stirring of emotions.
Who knows if this very moment
Somewhere in distant mountain
The snow at last may start to thaw.

Translated from Urdu by Pavan K. Varma

MOMIN

– Kailash Vajpeyi

There were houses of worship
Earlier too
There were killing fields as well
This is the progress
We have made
Now the two
Are one

Translated from Hindi by Ananya Vajpeyi

MONSOON CLOUDS BE MY MESSENGER

– Andal

Monsoon clouds you spread and spread
to hood earth, your torrent slashes
The sky, you shake the honey-heavy blossoms
of Vengadam hill and strew scented petals.
Go tell the dark lord who killed the demon Hiranya
ripping him with paws of fury
that he has robbed me of my bangles.
He must return them to me now.

Whirling clouds you enlarge in anger
and growl across the sky rending it open

with lightening. Spilling honey you tear
flowers, petals spatter like blood on earth.

Go to the fierce lord who roars and mauls
tossing his mane as his paws rip insides out.

Tell him I'm bloodied. He must heal
with long caresses, still me in his thrall.

Engorged with anger
nails extending he kills
plunging wrists in blood

from these very hands I seek
fondling
gather in my swollen ripeness

as spilling nectar
my body's bloodflower
bursts.

Translated from Old Tamil by Priya Sarukkai Chabria

MONSOON POEM

– Tishani Doshi

Because this is a monsoon poem
expect to find the words jasmine,
palmyra, Kuruntokai, red; mangoes
in reference to trees or breasts; paddy
fields, peacocks, Kurinji flowers,
flutes; lotus buds guarding love's
furtive routes. Expect to hear a lot
about erotic consummation inferred
by laburnum gyrations and bamboo
syncopations. Listen to the racket
of wide-mouthed frogs and bent-
legged prawns going about their
business of mating while rain falls
and falls on tiled roofs and verandas,
courtyards, pagodas. Because such
a big part of you seeks to understand
this kind of rain—so unlike your cold
rain, austere rain, get-me-the-hell-
out-of-here rain. Rain that can't fathom
how to liberate camphor from the vaults
of the earth. Let me tell you how little
is written of mud, how it sneaks up
like a sleek-gilled vandal to catch hold
of your ankles. Or about the restorative
properties of mosquito blood, dappled
and fried against the wires of a bug-zapping
paddle. So much of monsoon is to do
with being overcome—not from longing
as you might think, but from the sky's
steady bludgeoning, until every leaf
on every unremembered tree gleams
in the abyss of postcoital bliss.

Come. Now sip on your masala tea,
put your lips to the sweet, spicy skin
of it. There's more to see — notice
the dogs who've been fucking on the beach,
locked in embrace like an elongated Anubis,
the crabs scavenging the flesh of a dopey-
eyed ponyfish, the entire delirious coast
with its philtra of beach and saturnine
clouds arched backwards in disbelief.
And the mayflies who swarm in November
with all their ephemeral grandeur to die
in millions at the behest of light, the geckos
stationed on living room walls, cramming
fistfuls of wings in their maws. Notice
how hardly anyone mentions the word
death, even though the fridge leaks
and the sheets have been damp for weeks.
And in this helter-skelter multitude
of gray-greenness, notice how even the rain
begins to feel fatigued. The roads and sewers
have nowhere to go, and like old-fashioned pursuers
they wander and spill their babbling hearts
to electrical poles and creatures with ears.
And what happens later, you might ask,
after we've moved to a place of shelter,
when the cracks in the earth have reappeared?
We dream of wet, of course, of being submerged
in millet stalks, of webbed toes and stalled
clocks and eels in the mouth of a heron.
We forget how unforgivably those old poems
led us to believe that men were mountains,
that the beautiful could never remain
heartbroken, that when the rains arrive
we should be delighted to be taken
in drowning, in devotion.

English

MOTHER TONGUE
– Kedarnath Singh

As ants return to
their nests,
a woodpecker
returns to the wood,
and the airplanes return to the airport
one after another
stretching their wings in the red sky,

O my language,
I return to you,
when my tongue feels
stiff from
remaining silent,
hurting my soul.

Translated from Hindi by Kalpana Singh-Chitnis

MOUNTAIN CHILD
– Nirmala Putul

The mountain child—
a fragment of the mountain—
plays in the lap of the mountain

Toddling up the mountain
he plants his feet in the mountain soil
to rise like a mountain
in the land of mountains

The whole mountain
lives inside the mountain child
And in the lap of the mountain
lives the scurrying mountain child

The mountain child sees
a plane flying over the mountain
And he asks his father—
What is that bird?

Translated from Hindi by Lucy Rosenstein

MY EIGHT-ANNA COIN

– Vinod Kumar Shukla

My eight-anna coin
Is lost.
When I look for it
I find a silver rupee.
The rupee isn't mine,
But stamped on it
Is my severed head.
The rest of me must then be
In the eight-anna coin,
And that's why I've been
Desperately looking for it.
How was I to know
That my incomplete person
Would turn into
This money chase?

Translated from Hindi by Arvind Krishna Mehrotra

MY POEM
– Surjit Patar

My mother could not comprehend my poem
even though it was written in my mother tongue
She merely thought that some sorrow
plagued her son's soul

She wondered
where had this sorrow come from
when she was there all the time
to guard her son's soul

She scanned my poem with care
and exclaimed to herself
'Look, folks look!'
Instead of telling his mother
who gave him birth from her womb
the son chooses to tell his grief to paper

She held the paper to her bosom
hoping perhaps
that this may be the way
to reach out to her sorrowing son.

Translated from Punjabi by Nirupama Dutt

MY SISTER'S BIBLE
– S. Joseph

This is what my sister's Bible has:
a ration-book come loose,
a loan application form,
a card from the cut-throat money-lender,
the notices of feasts
in the church and the temple,
a photograph of my brother's child,
a paper that says how to knit a baby cap,
a hundred-rupee note,
an SSLC book.

This is what my sister's Bible doesn't have:
the preface,
the Old Testament and the New,
maps,
the red cover.

Translated from Malayalam by K. Satchidanandan

NEED
– Ramesh Chandra Shah

Now when everything is according to the season,
the temperature is just what it should be in these days
after a long time, the sky is breathing freely
and there is no one to reprimand the sun
then

why do I feel
as if something very precious
that I had
has been left behind
in that bad weather?
Why is it that for me alone
all directions
cover themselves with dust?
Why have the mountains
gleaming like a mirror till yesterday, turned alien to me?

What do I want, after all?
What is that need
that is neither
the farmer's
nor the potter's?

Translated from Hindi by the poet

NEGRO, MY BROTHER

– Ali Sardar Jafri

In this forest of ivory,
His black body,
Like a swirling black cloud,
Like a flash of black lightening,
A sea of black limbs,
That ebbs and flows and meanders,
Shining in the blazing sun,
Can turn into a spear,
Dancing to the beats of drums,
It takes on the enemy.
Negro, my brother,
Picks flowers from every forest.
My brother's feet are red,
Like roses.

Translated from Urdu by Baider Bakht and Kathleen Grant Jaeger

NIGHT'S GOLDEN WINEGLASSES
– Habba Khatoon

I've dyed my hands with henna.
When will he return to me?
While he roams distant lands, I'm dying—
my heart feels numb.

I've waited so long for him.
Now where's the delight in daylight?
Even night's golden wineglasses
grow dim.

But love's ritual remains sweet.
If only I could adorn my darling
with jewels, perfume his body,
and anoint him with my slippery kisses.

Although I'm torn apart inside,
love, thanks to you,
look across the lake.
That's the lotus of my heart in bloom.

Transcreated from Kashmiri by Abhay K. and Bill Wolak

NO, I AM NOT LOSING MY SLEEP
– Pash

No
I am not losing my sleep over
how and when
you'll strike
to finish me off
frankly, I couldn't care less
about it
because
I don't have the patience
of a watchman
to be on an eternal guard
to sift and filter
countless moments
to wait for
the time slot
your henchman have fixed for me?

No
I don't waste my time thinking about such trifles
nor am I sentimental about
the memories of my village
and the folks I left behind
No I don't think now about
such things as
the fine hues of red
when the sun sets over the village
nor do I care about
how she feels.

Translated from Punjabi by Suresh Sethi

NOT ENTIRELY HIDDEN
from *Cātu* Verses

Not entirely hidden
like the enormous breasts of those Gujarati women,
and not open to view,
like a Tamil woman's breasts
but rather
like the supple, half-uncovered breasts
of a Telugu girl,
neither concealed nor exposed:
that's how a poem should be composed.
Anything else
is a joke.

Translated from Telugu by Velcheru Narayana Rao and David Shulman

O MY FRIENDS
– Mirabai

O my friends,
What can you tell me of Love,
Whose pathways are filled with strangeness?
When you offer the Great One your love,
At the first step your body is crushed.
Next be ready to offer your head as his seat.
Be ready to orbit his lamp like a moth giving in to the light,
To live in the deer as she runs toward the hunter's call,
In the partridge that swallows hot coals for love of the moon,
In the fish that, kept from the sea, happily dies.
Like a bee trapped for life in the closing of the sweet flower,
Mira has offered herself to her Lord.
She says, the single Lotus will swallow you whole.

Transcreated from Rajasthani Hindi by Jane Hirshfield

O SAKHI, THE FLUTE PLAYS IN THE GROVE

– Salabega

O friend, tell me
who plays the flute
in the grove?
The bare trees bloom
at the sound of his flute.
The air stands still.
Stones turn into water.
The Yamuna flows upstream
and the fish seek the shore.
As the bell tinkles slowly,
freeing us from shame,
there's no time left to wear clothes.
Strange! the Rishi loses his poise
and succumbs to love.
The deer chases the tiger.
Says Salabega: I am Muslim by birth
But my heart is
at the feet of Radhakrishna.

Translated from Oriya by Sachidanand Mohanty and Smita Mohanty

ONLY A CONNOISSEUR

– Anon Baul

Only a connoisseur of the flavours of love can
comprehend the language of a lover's heart
others have no clue.
The taste of lime rests in the core of the fruit,
and even experts know of no easy way to reach it.
Honey is hidden within the lotus bloom—but the
bee knows it.
Dung-beetles nestle in dung, discounting honey.
Submission is the secret of knowledge.

Translated by Anon

ONLY ONE FACE
– Pankaj Chaturvedi

there is a famous statue
of Buddha in Kushinagar

seen from one angle it seems as if
Buddha is smiling
from a second angle he seems
lost in melancholic thoughts
from a third angle there is
the blessing of nirvana—
inviolable peace

do not think of this as the sum
of three expressions
Buddha could not just smile

his smile was melancholic
and in between
the radiance of desirelessness
or of the middle path

great the skill
that sculpted this stone
but greater still
the understanding of this art
which could discern
that in these three images there was
only one face of Buddha

Translated from Hindi by Rahul Soni

PATALIPUTRA

– Patumarattu Mocikiranar

Tell me, did you see him yourself,
or did you hear about it from someone
who had in fact seen him?
I just want to be sure.
May all of Pataliputra, swimming in gold,
where white-tusked elephants splash about
in the Sona River, be yours!
Tell me, again, from whose mouth
did you first hear of my lover's coming?

Pataliputra: Pataliputra, present-day Patna in Bihar, was the legendary capital of the Mauryan (321-185 BCE) and Gupta (320-550 CE) empires. Founded in 490 BCE by Ajatashatru, king of Magadha, it is located at the confluence of the Ganga and Son rivers.

Translated from Tamil by R. Parthasarathy

PATHS
– Salma

Upon the almirah
against the room's walls
between the swirling fan's blades
a bat clashes,
falls, scatters.

But birds, thousands of miles away
fly across the blue of the sky
and the massing of mountains
and have never, so far,
lost their way.

Translated from Tamil by Lakshmi Holmström

PEDRU UNCLE

– Hemant Divate

One by one your limbs turned traitor
Your wooden armchair
The ashtray in which you put out your *bidis*
Your shit-pot
The flutter of your faded Bible
And one frame of Christ is all that remains
I can still feel your presence
lying in the armchair, coughing and moaning
restlessly smoking *bidis*
Your life's becoming intolerable for you
But you can't restlessly
Pace about the room
Your lips tremble
but can't utter a word
Even the smoke trailing out of your *bidi*
seems as paralysed as you

In front of the framed Christ
mentally murmuring a prayer
your whole body is murmuring
Perhaps one last prayer for you and us
You used to ask everybody
'What do you do these days?'
At that time I was doing nothing
except writing poems
You used to say
'You are mad'
But you would read my poems
with great interest
You used to say
'When I was in college
I used to write poems
But that was because of madness

Poetry makes you weak, my son
The day I stopped writing
I stopped worrying about others
And I became the strongest man.'

All your life you were without a companion
All your life you remained an orphan
Nobody ever loved you

And now in a zero watt bulb's light
the words in the Bible must seem very faded
in the same way you too seem faded
to us all

From the bars of your window
you must be seeing
the day turning into night
You must be guessing the time by rough estimate
You can't expect anyone to arrive
And if at all you do wait for something
it is for the window and all the seasons you sense through it
to fall upon you like leaves
And when all by yourself
you would finally remember

your life
Silently
you would pray for Jesus
with an anguished soul
Uncle
You are nobody's relative
Whom will you remember?
And if you remember your life
what exactly was worth remembering in your life?

Now,
when I remember you I feel
I may be toppled down any moment myself

But
I am still holding on
Because I'm mad, Uncle,
I still write poems
I'm mad

Bidi: A cheaper cousin of cigarette made of unprocessed tobacco.

Translated from Marathi by Dilip Chitre

PEOPLE
– Tukaram

The deception was eating into me
so I started calling my dog 'God'.
He thought it was a bit loony
at first,
then he started to laugh, and even
danced a bit of a jig.
'Here God!' – he doesn't bite
any more. Now,
I wonder would
this work
with people?

Translated from Marathi by Anon

PIGEONS
– Bibhu Padhi

They embody a consciousness
that shines among light-grey rocks.
In their bodies old stories of flight
repeat themselves, refresh memory.
During the long Indian afternoons
they rest upon our polished floors,
their bodies refracting the warmth
of close contact, their small heads

forming a community of wisdom.
A picture of extreme importance is seen
a picture that comprehends everything,
all things contemporary and long past.
But before our eyes gain their fixed look
and our envy its pale green stare,
they rise up, holy and untouched,
to disappear in a history
of mocking wings,
in the accepting sky.

English

PLAY
– Ashok Vajpeyi

I spread out earth's green bed
I pull in sky's blue veil
I place sun and moon on two pillows
I remove grass's attire
I indulge in play with you.

Translated from Hindi by Sudeep Sen

PORTRAIT
– Dinkar Manwar

Don't turn away from me
Water
Stay within my sight
Don't babble or gush
Be utterly silent
Be utterly still

Let me enter deep into you
Let me at last hear your voice
Let me feel you with my desperate hands
Let my tongue lick your feet
Let me get a sense
Of what all you have been hiding in your heart

Water
My father my mother my lord
Wait for me for a while
I want to paint
Your portrait.

Translated from the Marathi by Sachin Ketkar

PRAISE GALORE TO THE LAND OF DHAT
– Rangrelo Bithu

The low hills are stony, russet and bare,
with no trees on them save the stunted thorny cactus.
You wouldn't hear the call of a peacock
in all the land.
Hyenas, porcupines and monitor lizards
are the only creatures that you'd come across.
The people are starved;
hunger drives them afield
in search of the prickly grass
whose seeds I have seen them eat.
Such as the Jadavs of Jaisalmer.

The senior queen drives her donkeys
to a distant pond to fetch her water;
alone she must go,
and bestirring with her hands
the water
to clear its surface
of the floating dirt and debris,
fill her pots;
and load them on to the wooden frames
on the donkey's backs
and drive them home,
trudging all the way,
tired and exhausted.

The king's chief bard is pot-bellied;
he wears his lower garment
in a loose unseemly manner;
he is lame in both his legs;
and groans at every step he walks.

The carpet on which the Rawal's court assembles
is worn, with large holes in it;
his poets are all stupid
and cannot distinguish between
a buffalo and an elephant;
to them coarse wool
and silk are just the same.
Such is the land of Dhat!
Praises be to the land of Dhat!

The comely women all go
to fetch water at dawn;
they return past midnight
dishevelled and distraught;
their dishevelled children
pine for them all day.
Such, indeed, is the land of Dhat!
Praises galore to the land of Dhat!

Dhat: heck, surprise

Translated from the Rajasthani by Kesri Singh

PRAYER
– Prabodh Parikh

Grant me the strength to look at you, to bear the radiance
of the sun;
the strength to alert faraway ships by my drumbeats,
to be a pearl diver,
to drive a toy-train,
to survive a famine,
to extract the magic potion from the tresses
of the femme-enfant.
Grant me, once more, an illusion.
And though I am no Socrates,
grant me the vision to hear, to swim
in the currents of the landscapes of French poets
which, half-open, float away in my blood.

Grant me an alphabet
of airplane and city,
which would let me sit by an ageing grandmother.
Grant me, once more, the illusion
of a ladder
to climb to You,
to me.

Translated from Gujarati by Naushil Mehta and Ranjit Hoskote

PUNDARĪKA

– Kshemendra

When he heard the news of his death
he stood without moving.
Then he let out a piteous cry
loud enough to break the stones of the mountains,
piercing his own life, rendering him unconscious.
O Pundarīka!
Even now, long past, when the deer remember it
they drop the grass from their mouths.

Punadarika: A legendary mythological figure in Hinduism described in *Skanda Purana* as an ascetic and devotee of God Vishnu.

Translated from Sanskrit by W.S. Merwin and J.M. Masson

RĀGHAVAPĀṆḌAVĪYA
– Kaviarāja

1.47

If you have not followed
the paths of poetry,
finding your way through the vines
and shoots of learning;
if the difficulty of word-weaving
is lost on you, with nothing decent to say
about the work of others;
if you haven't spent long hours
in the company of artists and aesthetes
who are you to make fuss
over my poems?

Transcreated from Sanskrit by Gabriel Rosenstock and Abhay K.

RUMI AND THE REED

– Tabish Khair

Listen to the song of the reed flute:
    It sings of separation.
Torn from the leaf-layered, wind-voiced
    Banks of the pond,
It is joined to sorrow and joy
    By a slender sound.
Who, asked Rumi, can understand
    The reed's longing to return?
        Let its raw lips rest then;
        Let all words be brief then.

And I, O Believers, cried Rumi
    (Having lost the man he loved),
I who am not of the East
    Nor of the West, un-Christian,
Not Muslim or Jew, neither
    Born of Adam nor Eve,
What can I love but the world itself,
    What can I kiss but flesh?
        Let my raw lips rest then;
        Let all words be brief.

English

SATYABHAMA

– Basudev Sunani

Satyabhama
Chuckled on the window seat
Of the bus, and then
Hid her face
In her hands

Was she shy?

Satyabhama
Faint, dark, like a slate,
Forgotten.

How could she
Have been otherwise?

It's two decades since
She was in class five
And I in two
In our village school.

On her cheek
The flush of self-confidence
To have learnt by rote
The alphabet.

Married to a dhoti-clad gentleman,
She is now in search
Of a suitable girl
For her son;

Persuaded by the villagers
She is now a candidate

In the local body election;

She said all this
Pressing her face
To the window-sill.

Satyabhama
Gives the feeling
Of someone intimate
Like the torn pages
Of an old book

From childhood

When eating porridge together
She taught me the art
Of sewing sal-leaf bowls.

There was nothing more
To share with Satyabhama.

By the time bus left
It seemed like
I was in class five
And she in class two.

I do not know
If I will meet her again.

If only I had had
A fleeting glimpse
Of her face.

Translated from Odia by Rabindra K. Swain

Abhay K.

SELECTIONS FROM *AMARUŚATAKA*

The house parrot overheard
the lovers' sweet nothings
all through the night,
when the sun arose
he spilled the beans;
members of the household
heard every syllable.
When she heard her own sweet words
the woman placed a ruby earring
in front of the bird, hoping he'd take it for
a pomegranate full of seeds –
bite into it and shut up. (16)

Love's chain has broken,
our friendship gone,
mutual respect and affection
wilted
he's just some other dude
strolling down the street.

But my eyes follow him, sweet friend,
I can't help admiring him
day in and day out:
how strange it is
that my heart
hasn't cracked open. (43)

Transcreated from Sanskrit by Gabriel Rosenstock and Abhay K.

SELECTIONS FROM *CHAURASPANCHASIKA*

– Bilhana

Even now
the woodcutter and fisherman turn home,
On his axe the moon and in his dripping net
caught yellow moonlight. The purple flame of fire
calls them to love and sleep. From the hot town
the maker of scant songs for bread wanders
to lie under the clematis flowers with his girl.
The moon shines on her breasts, and I must die . . .

Even now
I mind that I loved cypress and roses, dear,
the great blue mountains and the small grey hills,
the sound of the sea. Upon a day
I saw strange eyes and hands like butterflies;
For me at morning larks flew from the thyme
and children came to bathe in little streams . . .

Even now
I mind that the time of the falling of blossoms
started my dream into a wild life, into my girl;
Then was the essence of her beauty spilled
down on my days so that it fades not,
fails not, subtle and fresh, in perfuming
that day, and the days, and today.

A free interpretation from Sanskrit by E. Powys Mathers

Abhay K.

SELECTIONS FROM *GATHASAPTASATI*

Distance destroys love,
So does the lack of it.

Gossip destroys love,
And sometimes

It takes nothing
To destroy love. 81

In her first labour,
She tells her friends,
'I won´t let him
Touch me again.' They laugh. 123

'A scorpion's bitten her,' they cried,
And as she thrashed about,
Her shrewd friends in her husband's presence
Rushed her to her physician lover. 237

Bookish lovemaking
Is soon repetitive.
It's the improvised style
Wins my heart. 274

He groped me
For the underwear
That wasn't
There:

I saw the boy's
Fluster
And embraced him
More tightly. 351

He finds the missionary position
  Tiresome, and grows suspicious
If I suggest another.
  Friend, what's the way out? 476

Translated from Maharashtri Prakrit by Arvind Krishna Mehrotra. The numbers following the poems are according to Albrecht Weber's Das Saptaçatakam des Hāla (Leipzig: F.A. Brockhaus, 1881).

SELECTIONS FROM *THE RIGVEDA* AND *THE UPANISHADAS*

Gayatri Mantra

We meditate
on the glory of that Being
who has produced this universe
May He enlighten our minds.

Translated from Sanskrit by Swami Vivekananda

Pavamāna Mantra from *Bṛhadāraṇyaka Upaniṣad*

Lead us
from falsehood to truth
from darkness to light
from death to immortality.

Pavamāna: Purification

Shanti Mantra from *Bṛhadāraṇyaka Upaniṣad*

May all be happy
May all be healthy
May all see the good
May all be free from suffering.

Shanti: Peace

Vasudhaiva Kutumbakam
from *Maha Upanisad*

This is mine, that is yours
narrow-minded people think that way
For the noble-hearted
the whole world is a family.

Vasudhaiva Kutumbakam: The whole world is a family

Translated from Sanskrit by Abhay K.

SELECTION FROM *SADUKTIKARṆĀMṚTA*
– Śrīdharadāsa

She didn't even stop me
by saying, 'Don't leave!'
Nor did she ask -
"would I be away for long?"
She didn't weep long enough
to wet her cheeks
I was ready to depart
when she came
offering me a drink
for the road and placed
a fresh mango blossom
on my palm.
I could not move an inch. (923)

Transcreated from Sanskrit by Gabriel Rosenstock and Abhay K.

SELECTION FROM *ŚĀRṄGADHARAPADDHATI*
– Śārṅgadhara

As the bright day dawns
washing their podiums, they
gossip about politics and the antics
of the other sadhus,
they've been up till midnight
weaving their flowers and grass
for worship rituals.

Later, pretending to practice yoga
and austerities, they hang around
until they catch a glimpse of city girls
gently washing their supple breasts.

Thus these rogues
pass their time
by the river. (4028)

Transcreated from Sanskrit by Gabriel Rosenstock and Abhay K.

SELECTIONS FROM *SUBHĀṢITARATNAKOṢA*

– Silabhattarika

He was the first with whom I lay
and he is my husband now
Oh those moon-drenched nights!
A cooling breeze would come down from the slopes
carrying with it the drunken scent of jasmine.
I am who I was then, and yet I feel my heart
longing for that reed bank on the mountainside
that was witness to our loving and desire . . .
the whole night on fire. (815 | 24.9)

– Silhana

"They are flashes of lightning, sudden, snake-like,
and plunge us into darkness when they are gone.
Therefore let us forego the pleasures of the flesh
and cleave to the perfection of silence . . ."
How we belch out these words in cool, measured tones
shamelessly like foolish parrots:
Reciting, reciting, reciting until kingdom come. (1614 | 48.21)

Transcreated from Sanskrit by Gabriel Rosenstock

SELECTION FROM *SUBHĀṢITĀVALĪ*

– Vallabhadeva

The sun glows
like post-sacrificial embers
and rests a while on the western peaks,
the honeybee is sucked by sweetness
into the lotus, not knowing
the flower will close when light fails.

Those who earn money
with thought of profit only
cannot comprehend
their great loss. (1917)

Transcreated from Sanskrit by Gabriel Rosenstock and Abhay K.

SELECTIONS FROM *THERIGATHA*
– Mutta

Free, fabulously free
free from three trifles –
pounder, pounding bowl and my wicked lord
free from endless births and deaths
the chains that fettered me down
are suddenly no more.

– Sumangalmata

A woman set free at last, how free
how gloriously free I am from drudgery
of kitchen, harsh hunger pangs
the sound of empty pots,
free from that whimsical man
the spinner of yarns
peace at last

lust and hatred have gone
I rest under the shade of sprawling trees
and cherish happiness.

Transcreated from Pali by Abhay K. and Gabriel Rosenstock

SHADOW
– Brij Nath Betab

My own shadow
Overshadows my size,
Do I have a size?
I ask myself;

Does a migrant have some size?
I doubt it.

Translated from Kashmiri by the poet

SHAPES
– Chokhamela

The sugarcane is crooked
but not its juice.
The bow is curved
not the arrow.
The river is bent
but not its water.
Chokha is twisted
not his faith.
Why are you drawn
to the shape of a thing.

Translated from Marathi by Rohini Mokashi-Punekar

SILHOUETTE
– Adil Jussawala

Ravi asks me to wait, he'll give me a ride.
Delhi is quiet now, he'll give me a ride.
He saw many, taken in trucks, go for a ride.

A man with a face as flat as a hand
steps up and says, Keep Discipline,
Emergency means Discipline,
then falls back silent.

Across the street, on a terrace two stories high,
a silhouette
hits out and runs, hits nothing, runs.

Twenty years later, its feet broken,
will its hands fly to its face when a light's switched on?
Will it lie on a plank for days,
twisting a handkerchief?

It has my best wishes.

I wish it a straighter back, a strong earth,
I wish it a game that won't cripple.

Ravi studies his car-keys and is silent.
Clouds, not far, make a noise
like MiGs flying low.

There's silence, there's pain.

The boy continues his game
of make-believe cricket.

English

SITA'S TEARS
– Udayan Vajpeyi

Father is unhappy if I wander far from home alone. He buys me a cycle but doesn't let me ride it anywhere.

Every other day, grandmother's servant steals money from grandfather. He ignores the theft and concentrates on rowing the boat of his old age.

Mother tries to run the house with very little money. In order to pass journey, she reads *Ramcharitramanas* over and over again.

Then suddenly one day, as Sita sits in the Ashoka forest, the silhouette of father's sick face appears through her tears.

Translated from Hindi by Alok Bhalla

SON TO MOTHER

– Gnanakoothan

Get too chummy with girls
yours ears will dry up, you said.
If you are naughty
God will strike you blind, you said.
When I worried you for things to eat,
It's bad for your tummy, you said
I got you in exchange for a
winnow of bran, you said.
What a lot of lies, Mother, you told me
when I was young!
What made you stop?
Or did you think
I could survive with truth?
Perhaps you thought
lies for grownups were beyond your ken
and left it to the government
to rule by the law.
I don't like it.
Wean me, mother, when you like,
But feed me your lies
for all time.
You don't love me, don't you?

Translated from Tamil by Ashokamitran

SONG OF THE AVADHUT

– Dattatreya

Truly, it is by the grace of God
that the knowledge of Unity arises within.
Then a man is released at last
from the great fear of life and death.

All that exists in this world of forms
is nothing but the Self, and the Self alone.
How, then, shall the Infinite worship Itself?
Shiva is one undivided Whole!

The five subtle elements that combine to compose this world
are as illusory as the water in a desert mirage;
To whom, then, shall I bow my head?
I, myself, am the stainless One!

Truly, all this universe is only my Self;
It is neither divided nor undivided.
How can I even assert that it exists?
I can only view it with wonder and awe!

What, then, is the heart of the highest truth,
The core of knowledge, the wisdom supreme?
It is, "I am the Self, the formless One;
By my very nature, I am pervading all."

That one God who shines within everything,
who is formless like the cloudless sky,
is the pure, stainless, Self of all.
Without any doubt, that is who I am.

I'm the infinite and immutable One;
I'm pure Consciousness, without any form.
I don't know how, or to whom,
joy and sorrow appear in this world.

Translated from Sanskrit by S. Abhayananda (Stanza 1-7, Ch-1, Avadhut Gita)

SOUL SONG

– Abhay K.

I was always here
as blowing wind
or falling leaves
as shining sun
or flowing streams
as chirping birds
or blooming buds
as blue sky
or empty space
I was never born
I didn't die.

English

SUMMER

from Jayavallabha's *Vajjalagam*

Having burnt it all to ash
along with every animal,
the wild fire
shins up a dried-out tree
and surveys the forest again,
wondering what is left.

Translated from Prakrit by Martha Ann Selby

SUMMER AFTERNOON

–Vijay Deo Narayan Sahi

In the nearby bamboo grove
    a sudden chirping of birds

Perhaps the fat black cat
    I often saw on the parapet
        its tail upright
            is crossing the drain

Translated from Hindi by Arvind Krishna Mehrotra

SUNDORI
– Kynpham Sing Nongkynrih

Beloved Sundori,
Yesterday one of my people
Killed one of your people
And one of your people
Killed one of my people.
Today they have both sworn
To kill on sight.
But this is neither you nor I
Shall we meet by the Umkhrah River
And empty this madness
Into its angry summer floods?
I send this message
Through a fearful night breeze
Please leave your window open.

Translated from Khasi by the poet

TERMS OF SEEING
– E.V. Ramakrishnan

On our way home from school
We often spent hours in that abandoned
Orchard of mango, cashewnut
And tamarind trees, where each season had
Its fruit and each fruit tasted different.

There we raided the hidden hideouts
Of bootleggers, and broke their buried
Mud-pots. The crematorium in the corner
Revealed an occasional roasted vertebra.
Once we went further and discovered

A disused well, and peeped into its
Vaporous depths: the water smelt like freshly
Distilled alcohol. Through the clotted branches
Of close-knit shadows floated white
Turtles with glazed, metallic shells.

Moving with monastic grace, they looked
Knowledgeable, like much travelled witchcraft
Doctors. If they cast a spell, it was
Unintentional. As we bent down, their
Shaven heads rose and met a shaft of sudden

Sunlight at an angle, tilting the sun
Into the sea. Still, the light lingered over the hill
Like an intimate whisper of something
Forbidden. By this time, the terms of seeing
Were reset: the well was watching us now.

Its riveted gaze pierced us and even went
Beyond us. In the dark cornea of the well

The white turtles moved like exposed optic nerves.
And as if a word was spoken, we stepped
Back into the world of gravity, in silence.

English

THE ART OF COURTESAN

– Anon

I shall instruct you in lessons hierarchic
Passed on to me by my grandma, who had them from
her grandma
Who had received them from her grandma of the fourth
generation preceding.
Leaving out none of them I shall
Teach you all in the order of the Gurus.

The great grandma advised my grandma in secrecy
She in turn transferred them to my mother
Who practiced them and narrated
The same art to me. I shall
Disclose them to you in the order of the Gurus.

Darling, with a voice sweet as the veena and the cuckoo!
Womenfolk should amass as much wealth as possible
From their lovers when their youth is fresh
Thereafter they may live on
Only with their fallen breasts.

For a damsel with a rich bosom
Luxuriant hair, a sweet face
And radiant teeth flashing a smile
The pursuit of wealth is the real pursuit
Yet for that pursuit to bear fruit
Grandma's eyes should keep a watch.

When your eyes blackened and forehead adorned
After offering flowers to God
Wearing ornaments and chewing betel leaves
Go forth, with your maids
To face your crowded lovers with grace.

At the parlour you smile at one of them;
Accost another with a twist of your eyebrows, my daughter
Greet the third with a lowering of the brow
Welcome all others with your glances.

Inside the parlour, O pretty one!
Smile at one, flicker the eyebrows at another
Cast a sidelong glance at one, and nod at the others
Keep the world of lovers thus entertained.

Inside the parlour
Enchant everyone with the corners of your eyes
Making each of them feel you glance at him
Hovering like bees over a myriad lotuses.

Inside the parlour, O pretty one
With your versatile art of entertainment
Rouse desire in the mind of each
And perform to suit their varied whims,
So that they come again, once having gone.
Treat the visiting travellers with civility
Share pleasing secrecies with the lovers
Entertain the poets with betel leaves
Bow before the Brahmins; humour the lustful
Try to allure the high-born
Entice the family men
And blatantly flatter the capricious.

Grasp those who are sincere in love
Ensnare the noble ones with a show of affection
Win over the poets with a display of passion
Give food and clothes to maids
Respect greatly the man useful in future
Take you my counsel, my daughter.

Charm the celibate ones with words, the friends
The dependents with gifts

The family men with affected indignation
The lovers with bewitching glances
The foolish ones with tears of joy
The king with enticing charms
The sensualists with tact
The noble ones with a magic potion
The poets by lending your ears to their verses
And your own relations in other ways.

Translated from Malayalam by P. Narayana

THE BATTLEFIELD
– Kakkaipatiniyar Naccellaiyar

On the weak, shriveled arms of the old woman,
the veins stand out; her stomach is gnarled
as a blade of lotus. Unnerved by the fighting,
her son had turned his back on it. So folks whispered.
If he had fled in the heat of battle,
she thundered in a rage, these breasts that nursed him
I'll tear into pieces. Sword in hand,
she groped around in the bloodstained field,
turning over one lifeless body
after another. When she found her son
lying prostrate, hacked to death,
she rejoiced more than on the day he was born.

Translated from Tamil by R. Parthasarthy

THE BLACK MAN

– Ved Pal Deep

When I take a pen and a piece of paper
to collect the thoughts of my mind,
the picture of a black man
rises before my eyes.
His blood is red –

The blood of all humanity.
His thick, tufted and rough locks are
like an intertwined dense forest.
His muscles are strong as trees.
His white teeth produce
thunder and lightning;
At their very sight,
the glory of white civilization crumbles.
When I take up pen to write a verse
it becomes a gun
which a Negro of Congo
hangs on his shoulder,
somewhere in the deep dark wood,
under the cover of a tree,
to fire at the Belgian army.
When I have put down a word
in ink
on a piece of paper,
it becomes
a bright piece of diamond;
Its dusty ores
black hands sift out of deep earth,
underneath rugged plains and rocks,
to deck the crowns
in foreign lands.
When I move my lips

to sing songs,
I feel
tribes after tribes,
countless families of mankind,
like lions,
move out,
break their chains
behind the barbed fences of
the zoo,
built by their foreign masters.

Translated from Dogri by Balraj Puri

THE CORPSE

– J.P. Das

Someone's lifeless body lies in the street
surrounded by people.
Many simply walk past,
others cannot bear to look at it;
one's step falters, another falls silent,
and another shuts his eyes at the sight.

One passes by reciting mantras along the street;
for whom did this child pluck flowers?
Who laughed here,
who stretched out his arms
to put a halt to time,
and whose screams were lost
in the deserted street?

In the light's rush upstream,
someone was lost on the way; the heart's
many dreams were ground to ash.
Someone sighs deeply,
someone measures out life
with a burning candle,
and another finds his own way
in the half-light.

The people have all gone;
the street is deserted, laughter extinguished
in the end endlessness of space.
The corpse still lies in the middle of the street,
and I lie fast asleep on a lonely isle.

Translated from Oriya by Jayanta Mahapatra

THE COWHERD'S DAUGHTER
– Rūpa Gosvāmin

Oh friend, you
play in the mud like a child
your blouse not
even covering your breasts
your father, the cowherd
thinking you still a child
has done nothing
to find you a husband
but then suddenly
your eyelids leap as you hear
in the Vrindā forest the sound
of Krishna's flute
and you tremble with longing
and show the whites of your eyes.

Translated from Sanskrit by W. S. Merwin and J.M. Masson

THE DAY SHE WAS GONE

– Namdeo Dhasal

The day she was gone,
I painted my face black.
I slapped the savage schizophrenic wind hard in its face.
I picked up small pieces of my life
and stood naked in front of a cracked mirror.
I allowed myself to wreak vengeance upon myself.
I stared condescendingly at the Sun and said, 'You screwball!'
I showered choice curses upon all artists who paint dreams;
I walked from the East towards the West;
I picked stones I found on the way and hurled them at myself,
How boisterously flows this water in its fit of laughter
through mountains and gorges.
What ocean is it seeking to meet?
Or will it seep
into the soil at sea-level?
Did even I belong to myself?
I could not even embrace her dead body
and cry my heart out.
The day she was gone,
I painted my face black.

Translated from Marathi by Dilip Chitre

THE DESCRIPTION OF UMA'S LOVEMAKING
– Kalidasa

Shiva taught her how to make love
in their bed; Parvati offered him back
herself, full of grace of a young woman,
like a present one gives to one's guru

She trembled in pain as her bitten
lower lip was released slowly
Parvati took a deep breath of cool air
coming from the crescent moon in Shiva's hair

While kissing her long hair
dust fell into Shiva's third eye
Parvati blew it off with her perfumed breath
fragrant as the smell of a blossoming lotus

So the lord of the beasts whose mount is Nandi-
the Bull, gratifying Kama, the God of Love
by immersing himself in pleasures of senses
lived for a month with Uma in the Mountain King's palace.

Transcreated from Sanskrit by Abhay K. from Kumarasambhava 8.17-8.20

THE DIFFERENCE

– Akhtar-ul-Iman

How much I wept when I first realized
that someday I'll die and lose
the delight of all my pleasures,
even the ordinary ones:
pleasures like the hum of bees buzzing,
birds chirping, ravens weaving
straw nests in neem treetops,
tractor engines chugging along,
children playing in the dust,
and half-naked workers chewing on
dry pieces of bread and raw onions.
All these meaningless, ordinary joys
will suddenly vanish.
How much I wept when I first
felt this fear that my ties to the earth
will disappear, and I'll become
lifeless as stone.
But for a long time now my lips
have forgotten how to kiss,
and the exciting tumult of the heart
is a thing of the past,
causing in me this state of perpetual death.
And yet, my eyes haven't shed
even a single tear.

Transcreated from Urdu by Abhay K. and Bill Wolak

THE DOOR
– Anamika

I was a door
The harder they beat me
the wider I opened
They walked in and saw
a great cosmic whirling
When the grinding stops, the spinning begins
When the spinning stops, the sewing begins
Something or other, all day, non-stop

And in the end my broom sweeps it all up
sweeps up the stars in the sky
mountains, trees, stones
all the shards and splinters of creation
and collects them in a basket
stores them somewhere
deep inside
in some corner of the mind.

Translated from Hindi by Ritu Menon

THE EVENING
– Garikapati Pavan Kumar

Trees
black as mascara-touched
eyebrows of the beloved

the hill
sliding silently into
deep meditation

the sky
smiling with flushed cheeks.

That evening

in my room
engrossed in my work
with the loneliness
that has become a habit

like a prisoner

only the circling birds
feel happy…

Translated from Telugu by D. Kesava Rao

THE GLOW-WORM'S GLEAM
– Narain Shyam

There is a gleam of the glow-worm,
The night is dark and the journey long.
Light takes one step and darkness another
    There is a gleam of the glow-worm,
    The night is dark and the journey long.
Now here and now there,
flashes of light emanate.
    There is a gleam of the glow-worm,
    The night is dark and the journey long.
This light falls drop by drop but darkness
is a thirst.
    There is a gleam of the glow-worm,
    The night is dark and the journey long.
As you glance, now it glows and now it dies,
But the path darkens more and more,
    There is a gleam of the glow-worm,
    The night is dark and the journey long.
Perhaps one may complete this life's
pilgrimage only thus.
    There is a gleam of the glow-worm,
    The night is dark and the journey long.

Translated from Sindhi by D.K. Mansharamani

THE HERON

– Nannakaiyar

He said, "I am leaving, going away."
And I knew that once again
he was playing games with me.
"Get lost," I snapped at him.
"And don't bother coming back."

But where is he, my lord?
For only he can comfort me.
Tears fill the space between my breasts,
now a vast pond where white herons
with black legs stalk their prey.

Translated from Tamil by R. Parthasarathy

THE INSANE
– Vinda Karandikar

She slept with a cloud: and then, of course, she conceived;
The rest followed smoothly. The earthen pitcher at home
She smashed pleasurably and started on a body-ending pilgrimage.
On her way she met an ass whom she worshipped ceremoniously.
The left-over of the incense pot she secured greedily and said,
'If this too had turned into ashes what could I say to the world?
But Fate is overwhelming and walks ahead like a dog.'
Then she took some banyan leaves,
    and set them up on a peepal tree.
And said, 'Now I owe nothing to any man,
    not even as much as a full moon.'
The rest followed smoothly (This I mentioned earlier);
The Insane delivered a lightning;
    offering her breast to the lightning,
The Insane went ahead; on her way she met the Court Jester;
Then the King; then the Queen; then A; then B.
But the Insane was sane enough— she recognized none.

Translated from Marathi by the Poet

THE LEAF ON THE BRANCH
– Gulzar

It was perched on a branch;
Below were the waters of a lake,
And in it the reflection of the sky;
It was afraid of being drowned
But…
It neither swam, nor drowned, nor flew away
It just sat on the branch, and finally wilted…
One lone leaf on a branch!

Translated from Urdu by Pavan K. Varma

THE MAGICIAN

– Kamal Vora

The magician
pulled a rabbit out of his hat
and a dove from his jacket.
An orange appeared in his left hand
with the lost ring hidden inside it.

Whispering something with closed eyes
waving the magic wand,
he offered from his closed palm
whatever was asked for.
With a touch of his fingertips,
the pieces assembled
into a whole
one into two
two into many
Several into one.
What was visible just a second ago
vanished.

Afterwards, the conjuror continued chuckling.

From the crowd
one boy spoke up,
"Magician,
I'm frightened by your magic!
What if you turn me into a butterfly
that flutters away?"

The magician just continued laughing.
Then spreading his arms like wings,
he flew
right through the boy's eyes.

Translated from Gujarati by Dileep Jhaveri and Bill Wolak

THE MESSENGER SPEAKS TO RADHA

– Jayadeva

Krishna lingers
in the thicket
where together you mastered the secrets
of lovemaking.
Fixed in meditation,
sleepless
he chants a sequences of mantras.
He has one burning desire –
to draw *amrita*
from your offered breasts.

Sighs, short repeated gasps –
he glances around helpless.
The thicket deserted.
He pushes back in, his breath
comes in a rasp.
He rebuilds the couch of blue floral branches.
Steps back and studies it.
Radha, precious Radha!
Your lover turns on a wheel,
image after
feverish image.

She ornaments her limbs
if a single leaf stirs
in the forest.
She thinks it's you, folds back
the bedclothes and stares
in rapture for hours.
Her heart conceives a hundred
amorous games on the well-prepared bed.

But without you
this wisp of a girl
will fade
to nothing tonight . . .

Translated from Sanskrit by Andrew Schelling

THE NEED TO TRAVEL

– Sohini Basak

I cannot rhyme the green bird by my window
with the fan whirling, and my thoughts going backwards
in cycles homewards again. The few rooms that have been mine
I know by heart down to the turtle-shaped smudge
on the mirror, inspiration gathers like dust under the bed
saturated I wait for the night to fall. A screech of an owl
might tear it open, but the moon within the branches
is trapped in clichés. I confess my mind is a boomerang
that's fixed to a vocabulary of the familiar. Pinned
to my wall is the poetry of departures.
I should pack my bags now.

English

THE NEW MAN
– Anon Baul

Come, he greets you now.
The new man
has exchanged his possessions
for the knapsack
of a penniless rover.
Even as he dips into the Ganges
the name of Kali is on his lips.

A simple word
can shatter ignorance and disbelief:
Kali and Krishna are One.
The words are different
their meaning the same.
Breaker of word barriers
he truly
is borderless:
Allah, Jesus, Moses, Kali,
tycoon or pauper
the new man sees them One and the same.

Adrift in his heavenly musings
people take him for a lunatic.
He opens his arms wide
to embrace the world, calling all
to the ferryboat that's moored to life's shore.

Translated by Anon

THE ORIENTALIST
– Ranjit Hoskote

He went back to drafting policies of state
but never forgot the courtesan in the Sanskrit play.
She wrote him letters on pages folded
in triangles like betel leaves
but did not wait for the beloved and spring;
creepers soothed her, her lamp-lit hours passed
among the scented shadows of lovers.

English

THE SEA

– Sitanshu Yashaschandra

I have seen the ocean
before gods and demons simplified it.

I have seen water in the light
of polar submarine fire.
Fire and moisture are one.
To burn and to get wet are one and the same.

When I emerged from the sea
my palms held no pearls.
I am not a diver.
I am a poet.
That which is there, is there in my eyes.

Translated from Gujarati by E.V. Ramakrishnan

THE SECRET
– Joseph Furtado

Every year you blossom, tamarind,
and the sunbirds seek you as of old;
Every day gay children, tamarind,
come to romp around you as of old;
And, lo, every hour of the day
all these years I've waited, tamarind –
Silence! silence to the last, I pray;
It was all so fated, tamarind.
Pride consumes him, said they, tamarind,
And no pity had they, tamarind;
You the secret keep now, tamarind,
Keep it till all secrets are made known,
for I go to sleep now, tamarind,
till o'er all the trumpet's blown.

English

THE SLEEP
– Shankha Ghosh

When the sky washed clean the earth's face in the dark of night
None of us knew, we were all asleep.
When the grass blades danced with glee, holding each other
by waist
None of us knew, we were all asleep.
Rain did not descend within our deep sleep
Nor did we descend into the midst of rain. How then
Did the night's solitude, night's silence pass
And the languor of idle morning rise
Before our eyes…

None of us knew, we were all asleep.

Translated from Bengali by Kalyan Roy

THE TASTE OF IRON

– Dhumil

Look how words
are styled into a poem
Look at this
Read this man fallen amid letters.
You hear that?
Is it the clanging of iron or
the blood spilled on the soil?
Ask not the blacksmith
the taste of iron,
Ask the horse with a leash on his mouth.

Translation from Hindi by Kamalakar Bhat

THE TIGER
– Kavarpentu

"Where is your son?" you ask,
leaning against the fine pillar of my house.
I don't really know where he is.
This womb that bore him is now a desolate cave
a tiger once prowled around.
Go, look for him on the battlefield.

Translated from Tamil by R. Parthasarathy

THE UNICORN

– Suniti Namjoshi

I rode the wild unicorn,
in the green light of trees,
in the dark light of night,
past leaves and silver thorn,
in love and foul weather.
Love, will you ride with me?
But my love stayed behind,
far away behind me.
And I rode the wild unicorn
past love and foul weather.

English

THE WAY
– Bodhidharma

Earthlings while enjoying breath
worry themselves about death,
when replete they worry
have they enough to eat:
Great Uncertainty.
The past does not interest the sage,
who cares what comes in some future age.
Even the present cannot hold sway:
from second to second he follows the Way.

Transcreated from Sanskrit by Gabriel Rosenstock

THE YELLOW MUSTARD

– Amir Khusrau

The yellow mustard is blooming in every field,
Mango buds are clicking open, other flowers too;
The koyal chirps from branch to branch,
And the maiden tries her make-up,
The gardener-girls have brought bouquets.
Colourful flowers of all kinds,
in hands everyone's bringing;
But Aashiq-rung, who had promised to come
to Nizamuddin's house in spring,
hasn't turned up - it's been years.

The yellow mustard is blooming in every field.

Aashiq-rung: the lover
Koyal: Cuckoo

Translated from Persian by Anon

THE YOUNG WOMAN WHO SELLS FLOWERS
– Parimal Hansda

That young woman who, standing by the road
was selling flowers, today
She herself has turned into a
very beautiful flower

To suck the nectar of her body
like bumblebees, buzzing around her are so many
young men
Today, her address is
a hidden alley in the market
where, to fight her hunger,
she has turned her body into a shop

That young woman, when she stands at the bus terminus
or walks in the midst of people on the footpath
then, on spotting her, those very young men
avert their eyes and hide
behind the open ends of the saris of their women

That young woman is one of the many young women
And now she is not dependent on anyone anymore
She raises both her hands towards the sky
as if she knows that she would be able to touch and hold
the moving, glowing, blinking stars, planets, constellations

Sari: A garment worn by Indian women

Translated from Santhali by Hansda Sowvendra Shekhar

THEY BURNT MY FATHER AND GRANDFATHER

– K. Siva Reddy

They burnt my father and my grandfather
just next to this dust track.
Perhaps they burnt all the dead people in the village
just next to this dust track.
When we go along the dust track
we can still find broken pots, old winnowing baskets
and shrouds on the nearby date-palm trees.

Coming this far
after so long
it's become impossible not to shoulder a cremation ground.
If I wish to shift the burden on to another
he too is shouldering a cremation ground—
I am searching for one who hasn't turned into a cremation ground.

Translated from Telugu by M. Sridhar and Alladi Uma

THINGS OF BEAUTY
– Amrita Nair

I cannot do
Any of those beautiful things
Like ikebana
Or origami
Or embroidery.
But that's all right.
Because
I'm good at
Running into these same
Invisible walls
Repeatedly;
Because
There is nothing in this world
Half as beautiful
As a soul that hurtles
Towards
Its own shattering.

English

THIRST

– Sahir Ludhianvi

World of palaces, crowns and thrones,
What does society care for this day?
A world that measures all that it owns:
What's this world should it come my way?

Injured body, thirsty soul,
Restless glance, the heart afraid,
What world is this? A senseless hole:
What's this world should it come my way?

Playing with people like some wooden toy
Is it life we worship...or is it the grave?
Is it sorrow we seek...or maybe pure joy:
What's this world should it come my way?

Wandering youth in search of hope,
So many bodies up for sale,
Love exchanged for a measly grope:
What's this world should it come my way?

World where man is no more than dust
Loyalty nothing, friendship a game
Love melts so easily into lust:
What's this world should it come my way?

Burn it all on a funeral pyre
Remove this world from me in a blaze
Set it on fire, set it on fire:
What's this world should it come my way?

Transcreated from Urdu by Gabriel Rosenstock

THIS HELPLESSNESS
– Shamsher Bahadur Singh

This helplessness
    sometimes becomes moon
    sometimes black palm
    a wall, a dam
    a flash of lightning that
    seems to caress the mountain every moment.

This helplessness
    turns simple living
    into a storm of blood.
This helplessness
    is fathomless
    even in silence.

Emotions become a cross
    raised as shoulders
    unbending.
    The joints of bones
    are loosening.
Tears break out of the dreams of lightning:
the earth is dry as the eye.

In the disturbed depths is immense
    silence.

Translated from Hindi by Nalini Taneja

TIBET

– Uday Prakash

Having come from Tibet,
Lamas keep wandering around
These days, mumbling mantras

Their herds of mules
Go down into the gardens
They do not eat marigold flowers

How many flowers
On one marigold plant,
Papa?

When it's the rainy season
in Tibet,
What season
Do we have?

When it's three o'clock
In Tibet,
What time
Is it here?

In Tibet
Are there marigolds,
Papa?

Do lamas blow conch shells, Papa?

Papa,
Have you ever seen lamas
Wrapped in blankets
Running quickly
In the darkness?

When people die
Lamas stand
On all four sides of the graves
And bow their heads

They do not recite mantras.

They whisper—tibbut
tibbut tibbut
tibbut tibbut
tibbut tibbut
And they cry
all night long.

Do lamas
Cry just
Like us, Papa?

Translated from Hindi by Robert A. Hueckstedt

TIME
– Kambadasan

The flame of the bed-chamber lamp
turned red like a newt's tail,
trembled before the rushing breeze
The book slipped from my hands,
I hastened to close the window
Out in the sky
in the poison-black night
countless stars
throbbed with light
Inwardly I trembled
like a trapped fish.
I was all ears
electrified by flute-music
Sweet desire welled up
and touched
my inmost being
like a prisoner bound
like a bee intent on honey
I followed the music's trail
to reach
that daunting crematorium
where I saw
the lone figure of man
As he poured forth
melodies from his flute,
a hooded serpent appeared.
Terrified I cried,
'Look, a deadly snake!'

Was he deaf?
He never moved but
flooded the world

with music from the flute
through his pining breath
All my mounting fears
vanished without a trace
As the first streak of dawn
oozed like milk
from the black pot of night,
I gazed upon his countenance.
Lo! he was blind—
I blind to the world
But he
like a dark cloud,
moved on, raining music
all the way.

Translated from Tamil by N.V. Rajamani

TIME DOES NOT PASS

– Rajendra Bhandari

Baje has become incapable of going down to the fields
Last year, using a stick, he could reach the yard
This time he only made it to the porch
After a three-day confinement, Baje passed away.
Boju passed away
Then mother began to pass away
At first she passed from the yard to the porch
At the porch she became a scarecrow to the grain
drying in the yard
The light passed from her eyes,
from her legs, the strength to stand
even as her desires were passing,
she passed away herself.
One day, a wild young thing flirted with me
But like a calm lake, I pooled by her side
Youth was passing from me
In the yellow autumn, in the fields
the paddy was passing into haystacks
the grain had passed and become manure
The world itself is passing every day
The atmosphere is passing into the ozone hole
With the passing of seedling, and of plant
the passing of flower and dead leaves
the passing of leaf and shoot
the passing of bud and flower
with these passages
the venerable lotus passed from the face of the earth
But time has not passed
Time is just not there
Time would pass, if at all it existed.

Baje: Grandfather
*Boju:*Grandmother

Translated from Nepali by Anmole Prasad

TO HER BESTIES
– Vidyā

How lucky you're all that you recall
the games you played with your lovers,
those moans and laughter, syllables of sweet pain
When my lover unknotted my dress
I swear I remember nothing afterwards.

Translated from Sanskrit by Abhay K.

TRAFFIC JAM

– Nilim Kumar

As I drive out from home
suddenly I forget
where I was headed to
When I get stuck
in traffic jams in a hurry
then I feel restless
and I remember
where I was headed to

Many people tell me –
'I saw you the other day
in the traffic jam'

Yes!
Who was it that saw me in the traffic jam?
I have to enter into another traffic jam
to remember.

Translated from Assamese by Bibekananda Choudhury

WASN'T IT WOMAN WHO BORE THEM
– Sanchiya Honnamma

Wasn't it woman who bore them
Wasn't it woman who raised them
Then why do they always blame woman,
These boors, these blind ones.

In the womb they are the same
When they are growing they are the same
Later the girl will take, with love, what's given
The boy will take his share by force.

For money's sake, for trust
and friendship's sake
Don't give a girl to a walking corpse
bereft of virtue, youth and looks.

Don't say, "We are poor people, where
can we get jewels from?"
Instead of spending on yourself
provide your daughters with clothes and ornaments.

Translated by Tejaswini Niranjana from Kannada

WHAT BLUE IS

– Binoy Majumdar

I do not swallow my miracle flower in an instant
Like chocolate, I suck it slowly for pleasure
Forgetting my age-old thirst in discovery and love.
I have reflected, with many snakebites on my heart,
Known what it is to be rent apart, what blue is—
In the sky, in the heart; what an impassive bird is.
Or the dragonfly soars on its transparent wings.
Its breath still warm on the young man's heart.
Illness enchants me, I watch the scene at the window
Where the sky drools in the shelter of the wind.
I am entranced, you've flown away; come back, wheel
As the chariot, as victory, as eternal poetry.
We will sing in a pure land, we will be love,
As faceless melody, we will daub all the skies.

Translated from Bengali by Arunava Sinha

WHAT FRENZY IS THIS?

– Zareef Ahmed Zareef

My gaze has been silenced
What frenzy is this?
I lost the city of love I'd found,
What frenzy is this?

I worshiped shadows all my life
Did I alone miss
the arrival of the dawn
What frenzy is this?

I smeared the glass with blood
to make mirrors
My image—a stranger
What frenzy is this?

I couldn't read
the writing on floral walls
my lines of fate turned mute
What frenzy is this?

Socrates did me no favour in leaving
I shouldn't be saying this, but
He didn't drink my share of poison
What frenzy is this?

I've lost the city of love I'd found,
What frenzy is this
My gaze has been silenced
What frenzy is this?

Translated from Kashmiri by the poet

WHEN IT RAINS IN DHARAMSHALA
– Tenzin Tsundue

When it rains in Dharamshala
raindrops wear boxing gloves,
thousands of them
come crashing down
and beat my room.
Under its tin roof
my room cries from inside
and wets my bed, my papers.
Sometimes the clever rain comes
from behind my room,
the treacherous walls lift
their heels and allow
a small flood into my room.
I sit on my island-nation bed
and watch my country in flood,
notes on freedom,
memoirs of my prison days,
letters from college friends,
crumbs of bread
and Maggi noodles
rise sprightly to the surface
like a sudden recovery
of a forgotten memory.
Three months of torture,
monsoon in the needle-leafed pines
Himalaya rinsed clean
glistens in the evening sun.
Until the rain calms down
and stops beating my room
I need to console my tin roof
who has been on duty
from the British Raj.

This room has sheltered
many homeless people.
Now captured by mongooses
and mice, lizards and spiders,
and partly rented by me.
A rented room for home
is a humbling existence.
My Kashmiri landlady
at eighty cannot return home.
We often compete for beauty
Kashmir or Tibet.
Every evening,
I return to my rented room;
but I am not going to die this way.
There has got to be
some way out of here.
I cannot cry like my room
I have cried enough
in prisons and
in small moments of despair.
There has got to be
some way out of here.
I cannot cry,
my room is wet enough.

English

WHEN YOU COME
– Anupama Basumatary

Whenever you come
I stay rooted, still,
a tree standing
mute sculpture.

This hour of meeting you
is bright as day
green as grass.

Yet, sure as death
is our parting.

Translated from Assamese by Pradip Acharya

WHERE THE MIND IS WITHOUT FEAR
– Rabindranath Tagore

Where the mind is without fear and the head is held high
Where knowledge is free
Where the world has not been broken up into fragments
by narrow domestic walls
Where words come out from the depth of truth
Where tireless striving stretches its arms towards perfection
Where the clear stream of reason has not lost its way
into the dreary desert sand of dead habit
Where the mind is led forward by thee
into ever-widening thought and action
Into that heaven of freedom let my country awake.

Translated from Bengali by the poet

WHILE I SLEPT
– Navtej Bharati

Time aged me
while I slept
I will not forgive it
for this treachery
I will not accept this old age
grafted slyly on my body
I will hide in the
leaves of grass
in the drops of water.
Will slip away
from its wrinkled hands.

Translated from Punjabi by the poet

WHIRLWIND
– Ravji Patel

When I'd finished my bath
I wiped my body
with the smell of the green fields.

The moment I whistled,
cows jumped in
through the window
carrying the morning's sunshine
on their horns,

buffaloes jumped in
their bodies slick
with the waters of the lake
foul with fish-smells,

goats jumped in
with lonely roads,
the muddy edges of roads
deserted fields
and peacock feathers
in their eyes,

I jumped in,
a whirlwind in the house.

Translated from Gujarati by Hansa Jhaveri

WHO WAS IT?
– Shahryar

Who was it, who was it
Who broke the spell of the city of dreams
Who clanged every chord of my soul
Who abandoned me in the arms of emptiness

It wasn't the merciless sky
Nor was it the confidante of my sorrows
It wasn't my poor, frail body
Then who was it?

Translated from Urdu by Rakshanda Jalil

WHY MARRY?
– Vemana

Why would you marry, have children,
call woes down upon yourself?

It defies logic—

Like hoisting
a boulder
from the earth
    to bear
    upon
    your
    head.

We know all about it when a rich man has a rash,
but whoever hears about a poor man's nuptials?

Transcreated from Telugu by Amanda Bell

WINTER
– Bijoy Sankar Barman

Shrouded in fog
is the distant red hillock
A tree
leans over the river

Canoes glide over the rapids
Night buries the sighs of dusk

In the lonely house
emptied by the last autumn wind
an old violin has so long remained
covered in dust

Last night
after the rain I saw
a shadow lying by my head
on the floor

Was it mine

Translated from Assamese by Nirendra Nath Thakuria

WITHIN
– Basavanna

Say now, what good is it
if a parrot can read aloud
but cannot hear the cat approaching
or if an eye can see the world
not knowing that the eye is squinting?
They say they know the world and all its sin
And fail, O Lord, to look within!

Translated from Kannada by Laxmi Chandrashekar and Vijaya Guttal, reworked by Gabriel Rosenstock

WITHOUT MY BODY

– B.B. Agarwal

When I returned home this evening
a strange incident happened :
nobody noticed me.
My wife did not ask me for tea
my children too kept away from me
my servant, showing great impertinence
kept on cleaning the floor
as if I did not exist.
Well, am I here or not?

Suddenly, then, I realize
with a feeling of great astonishment.
My body is missing.
I want to switch on the radio –
my hands are missing.
I want to speak –
my mouth is gone!
I have vision, alas! no eyes.
I can think – but my head is missing
So...
How have I returned home?

Slowly I started to understand:
I left my mind in the office accidentally while heading home.
My hands still hanging from the bus-strap.
My eyes still scanning the office files;
my mouth stuck to the telephone.
And my feet left standing in a queue, no doubt.
That's how I returned home today, without my body.

Vision of a bodiless life
is the essence of Indian philosophy
But is the exhaustion weighing down the bodiless me
also a part of it all?

Translated from Hindi by Abhay K.

YOU
– Ismail

You're mine
only when you take off all your clothes
for me

When you're dressed
you belong to the world

I'm going to shred this world
into pieces
one day

Translated from Telugu by Velcheru Narayan Rao

YOU AND I
from *Kuruntokai*

My mother and yours, what are they to each other?
my father and yours, how are they kin?
You and I, how do we know each other, and yet somehow
like water raining down on red earth
our loving hearts have mingled.

Translated from Tamil by George L. Hart

YOU ARE THAT

from the *Chhandogya Upanishad* VI. I2. 1-3

Uddalaka asked his son to fetch a banyan fruit.

'Here it is, Lord!' said Svetaketu.
'Break it,' said Uddalaka.
'I have broken it, Lord!'
'What do you see there?'
'Little seeds, Lord!'
'Break one of them, my son!'
'It is broken, Lord!'
'What do you see there?'
'Nothing Lord!' said Svetaketu.
Uddalaka said: 'My son! This great banyan tree
has sprung up from seed so small
that you cannot see it.
Believe in what I say, my son!
That being is the seed; all else
but His expression.
He is truth. He is Self.
Svetaketu! You are that.'

Translated from Sanskrit by Shree Purohit Swami and W.B. Yeats

YOU CANNOT OWN SOMEONE
– Firaq Gorakhpuri

Nobody has ever belonged to someone for a whole lifetime
You cannot own someone
The beauty that you see with your eyes and the love that you feel
are only the illusions of the mind
All my life I have tried to save myself from
the glances of your eyes
Even then I failed and the dagger went
right through me.

Translated from Urdu by the poet

YOU WOULD HAVE BEEN A SAINT
– Ghalib

Ah, Ghalib, the magic of your words and your ways with mystics!
You would have been a saint – if you were not addicted to drink.

Translated from Urdu by Gulzar

YOUR THOUGHTS

– Raghuvir Sahay

How confidently you express my thoughts, even if inaccurately!
I never had the self-assurance to do so,
even when I hoped I might be right.
I never raised my voice—assumed that the right
to do so was mine alone, but lacking thoughts of your own
you have stolen mine,
and how authoritatively you trumpet them!
I suppress a little grin, try to conceal my amusement from you,
so as to save my thoughts from your misrepresentation.
I keep them to myself, for my own expression—
let you lose yourself down some blind alley.

Transcreated from Hindi by Amanda Bell

YOUR TRUST
– Om Nagar

How fast collapses
your trust
like a pack of cards

If I had met you at the grocery shop
I would have put two handfuls of trust long ago
in your wounded palms

like sand castles
your trust collapses
as soon as I withdraw my feet

you throw in the sky with your hands
walls, verandahs and those little windows
where you place an earthen lamp every night to light up inside

sometimes your trust perches on the top of date-palms
and I start digging shadows,
deeper I dig, deeper the trust grows.

Translated from Rajasthani by Abhay K.

ACKNOWLEDGEMENTS

I would like to thank Gabriel Rosenstock without whose support and encouragement this anthology would not have seen the light of day.

I want to thank Dipanjali for designing a great cover for this anthology. I would like to thank Rajiv Beri, Paul Vinay Kumar, Jyoti Mehrotra, Rajbilochan Prasad and Satyabrat Mishra of Bloomsbury India for their constant support and belief in this book. I wish to thank Shelly Bhoil for carefully going through the text and making valuable suggestions.

I take full responsibility for any error that might have inadvertently crept into the anthology.

PERMISSIONS ACKNOWLEDGMENTS

All the poems included in the anthology have been voluntarily contributed by the poets and/or their respective translators. Permission to include the poems has been granted by the individual poets, translators and publishers. If through inability to trace the present copyright owners, any copyright material is included for which permission has not specifically been sought, apologies are tendered in advance to proprietors and publishers concerned. Every effort has been made to trace individual copyright-holders. This has not been possible for every poem; therefore, the publisher will be happy to make the necessary amendments at the first opportunity.

'This Homage We Pay' (*Uttararāmacarita* of Bhavabhūti 1.1), transcreated from Sanskrit by Gabriel Rosenstock and Abhay K., used by permission of Gabriel Rosenstock and Abhay K.

'A Love Poem from India: Author's Consent' by Mahe Jabeen, translated from Telugu by Velcheru Narayan Rao, used by permission of Mahe Jabeen and Velcheru Narayan Rao.

'A Marvel' by Anon, translated from Sanskrit by W.S. Merwin and J.M. Masson, used by permission of J.M. Masson.

'A New Way of Waiting' by Shakunt Mathur, translated from Hindi by Aruna Sitesh and Arlene Zide, used by permission of Arlene Zide.

'A Poem' by Mir Taqui Mir translated by E. Powys Mathers from *The Garden of Bright Waters: One Hundred and Twenty Asiatic Love Poems*. Available in public domain.

'A Poem Never Says Anything' by Uttaran Chaudhuri, translated from Bengali by the poet, used by permission of Uttaran Chaudhuri. First appeared in *The Journal of Poetry Society of India*, Vol. 23, 2012.

'After the Curfew' by Nida Fazli, translated from Urdu by Nirupama Dutt, used by permission of Nirupama Dutt.

'Again Snowfall' by Jiban Namdung, translated from Nepali by Jas Yonjan 'Pyasi'.

'Alphabets' by Nabaneeta Dev Sen, translated from Bengali by Nandana Sen, used by permission of Nabaneeta Dev Sen and Nandana Sen.

'Ambapali' by Vishwanath Prasad Tiwary, translated from Hindi by Sunita Jain, used by permission of Vishwanath Prasad Tiwary and Sunita Jain.

'Amrutlal' by Udayan Thakker, translated from Gujarati by the poet, used by permission of Udayan Thakker.

'An Asian Child Enters a British Classroom' by Debjani Chatterjee, previously published in Debjani Chatterjee's collection *Do You Hear the Storm Sing?* (Core Publications, London, 2014), used by permission of Debjani Chatterjee.

'An Invitation' by Vallana, transcreated from Sanskrit by Amanda Bell, used by permission of Amanda Bell.

'An Orange' by Jibananada Das, translated from Bengali by Arunava Sinha, used by permission of Arunava Sinha.

'And Death Demands a Labor' by Sumita Chakraborty, used by permission of Sumita Chakraborty.

'Apparition on the River Bank' by Bhojya Deva transcreated from Sanskrit by by Bill Wolak, used by permission of Bill Wolak.

Ashtavakra Gita Ch-I translated from Sanskrit by Bart Marshall, used by permission of Bart Marshall.

'Aubade' by R. Parthasarathy, *Kavya Bharati*, 16 (2004). Copyright © 2017 by R. Parthasarathy, used by permission of R. Parthasarathy.

'Aubade' by Jayshankar Prasad, translated from Hindi by Romila Thapar, used by permission of Romila Thapar.

'Bardic Stuff' by Manohar Shetty, used by permission of Manohar Shetty.

'Bars' by Keki N. Daruwalla, used by permission of Keki N. Daruwalla.

'Beggar' by Angshuman Kar, translated from Bengali by Dr Ajoy Ranjan Biswas, used by permission of Angshuman Kar and Dr Ajoy Ranjan Biswas.

'Birthplace with Buried Stones' by Meena Alexander, from *Birthplace with Buried Stones* (Northwestern University Press) Copyright © 2013 by Meena Alexander. Used by permission of Meena Alexander.

'Black Bag' by Pavankumar Jain, translated from Gujarati by Arvind Krishna Mehrotra; used by permission of Arvind Krishna Mehrotra

'Bone of Time' by Jayanta Mahapatra, used by permission of Jayanta Mahapatra.

'Breasts' by Kutti Revathi, translated from Tamil by Lakshmi Holmström, used by permission of Kutti Revathi, Mark Holmström and Radhika Holmström.

'Breath' (Poem 52) by Lal Ded, translation(c) Ranjit Hoskote from Kashmiri; used by permission of Ranjit Hoskote. First appeared in I, Lalla: The Poems of Lal Ded (New Delhi: Penguin Classics, 2011).

'Buddha on the Highway' by Kalpatta Narayanan, translated from Malayalam by K. Satchidanandan, used by permission of Kalpatta Narayanan and K. Satchidanandan.

'Champa' by Katyayani, translated from Hindi by Nirupama Dutt, used by permission of Nirupama Dutt.

'Chill Out' by Anon, transcreation by Gabriel Rosenstock and Abhay K., original language: Gondi, used by permission of Gabriel Rosenstock and Abhay K.

'Cities of Memories' by Sunil Gangopadhyay, translated from Bengali by Kalyan Roy and Bonnie MacDougall.

'Consistently Ignored' by GS Sharat Chandra.

'Conversation Piece' by Eunice de Souza, used by permission of Eunice de Souza.

'Dance of Shiva' by Hoshang Merchant, used by permission of Hoshang Merchant.

'Daring' by Padma Sachdev, transcreated from Dogri by Amanda Bell, used by permission of Amanda Bell.

'Dawn in Winter' by Agyeya, translated from Hindi by Lucy Rosenstein, used by permission of Lucy Rosenstein.

'Day After Day' by Annamaya, translated from Telugu by Velcheru Narayana Rao and David Shulman, used by permission of Velcheru Narayana Rao and David Shulman.

'Death of a Rogue Elephant' by N. N. Kakkad, translated from Malayalam by E.V. Ramakrishnan, used by permission of E.V. Ramakrishnan.

'Deception' by Sampurna Chattarji, used by permission of Sampurna Chattarji.

'Description of the Missing One' by Kunwar Narain, translated from Hindi by Apurva Narain, used by permission of Apurva Narain.

'Digamabara' by Anitha Thampi, translated from Malayalam by K. Satchidanandan, used by permission of Anitha Thampi and K. Satchidanandan.

'Do Not Ask' by H.S. Shivaprakash, translated from Kannada by the poet, used by permission of H.S. Shivaprakash.

'Dothead' by Amit Majmudar, used by permission of Amit Majmudar.

'Easy, Friend' by Kabir, translated from vernacular Hindi by Arvind Krishna Mehrotra, used by permission of Arvind Krishna Mehrotra.

'Engraving of a Bison on Stone' by Arvind Krishna Mehrotra, used by permission of Arvind Krishna Mehrotra.

'Epitaph' by Mohammad Alvi, translated from Urdu by Anisur Rahman.

'Epitaph' by Shakti Chattopadhyay, translated from Bengali by Arvind Krishna Mehrotra, used by permission of Arvind Krishna Mehrotra.

'Epitaph on My Gravestone' by Manushya Puthiran, translated by C.S. Lakshmi and Arundhati Subramaniam, used by permission of Manushya Puthiran, C.S. Lakshmi and Arundhati Subramaniam.

'Every Land Our Home' by Kaniyan Punkunran, Weber Studies 15.1 (Winter 1998), translated from Tamil by R. Parthasarathy, Copyright © 2017 by R. Parthasarathy, used by permission of R. Parthasarathy.

'Exile' by Ravi Shankar, used by permission of Ravi Shankar.

'Eyes' by Vasant Abaji Dahake, translated from Marathi by Ranjit Hoskote, used by permission of Ranjit Hoskote.

'Famine and After' by Nagarjuna, translated from Hindi by Nalini Taneja, used by permission of Nalini Taneja.

'Farewell' by Jiban Narah, translated from Assamese by Lyra Neog, used by permission of Lyra Neog.

'Father Returning Home' by Dilip Chitre, translated from Marathi by the poet. Used by permission of Vijaya Chitre.

'Forest Ballads' by Niranjan Chakma, translated from Chakma by Udayan Ghosh.

'Four Haiku and a Tanka' by K. Ramesh, used by permission of K. Ramesh.

'Friends, This Is the Only Way' by Sachal Sarmast, translated from Sindhi by Ivan M. Granger, used by permission of Ivan M. Granger.

'Frogs' by Buddhadev Bose, transcreation from Bengali by Bill Wolak, used by permission of Bill wolak.

'Giant Buildings' by Munibur Rahman, transcreation by Gabriel Rosenstock and Abhay K., original language: Urdu, used by permission of Gabriel Rosenstock and Abhay K.

'Girls on Rooftops' by Alok Dhanwa, translated from Hindi by the poet, used with the permission of Alok Dhanwa.

'God' by Anuradha Mahapatra, transcreation from Bengali by Bill Wolak, used by permission of Bill Wolak.

'Grandfather's Photograph' by Mangalesh Dabral, translated from Hindi by Arvind Krishna Mehrotra, used by permission of Mangalesh Dabral and Arvind Krishna Mehrotra.

'He Is a Poet' by Shankar Ramani, translated from Konkani by Damodar Mauzo, used by permission of Damodar Mauzo.

'He Promised He'd Return Tomorrow' by Vidyapati, translated from Maithali by Azfar Hussain, used by permission of Azfar Hussain.

'Here Comes God' by Tenetti Suri, translated from Telugu by Velcheru Narayan Rao, used by permission ofVelcheru Narayan Rao.

'History of Justice' by Rohan Chhetri, used by permission of Rohan Chhetri.

'Horse Play' by K. Ayyappa Paniker, translated from Malayalam by K. Satchidanandan, used by permission of K. Satchidanandan.

'How can a River Reject its Fish' by Janabai, transcreated from Marathi by Bill Wolak, used by permission of Bill Wolak.

'How to Go to the Tao Temple' by K. Satchidanandan, translated from Malayalam by the poet, used with the permission of K. Satchidanandan.

'How to Read a Book' by Muddupalani, translated from Telugu by Velcheru Narayan Rao and David Shulman, used by permission of Velcheru Narayan Rao and David Shulman.

'How to Tame a Pair of New Chappals' by Gopal Honnalgere. Internodes, Samkaleen Prakashan, 1986.

'I have Brought the Sacrificial Goat' by Joy Goswami. From *Selected Poems: Joy Goswami* translated from Bengali by Sampurna Chattarji (Harper Perennial, 2014). Used by permission of Sampurna Chattarji.

'I Have Given Birth to a Son' (Tribal birth song by a Bhil mother), translated from Bhili by Abraham Thuruthumalil, *Dharmaram Journals, Poetry of Indian Tribals*, Volume 17, Issue 2.

'I Wear My Wordlessness' by K. Srilata, used by permission of K. Srilata.

'Ice Cubes, Cake & Roti' by Souvik Bandopadhyay, translated from Bengali by Neelav Bose, first appeared in the journal of the Poetry Society of India vol. 23, 2012, used by permission of Souvik Bandopadhyay and Neelav Bose.

'Imaginary Number' by Vijay Seshadri, used by permission of Vijay Seshadri.

'In Her Lovemaking She Grieves' by Gagan Gill, translated from Hindi by J.P. Das, Arlene Zide and Madhu B. Joshi, used by permission of Gagan Gill, J.P. Das and Arlene Zide.

'In the Dust Forever' by Tarannum Riyaz, translated from Urdu by Miraan Punjabi, used by permission of Tarannum Riyaz.

'In the Event of Change' by Tsering Wangmo Dhompa, used by permission of Tsering Wangmo Dhompa.

'Incurable by Yaquin', translated from Urdu by Edward Powys Mathers, available in public domain.

'Jaisalmer – IV' by Gulammohamed Sheikh, translated from Gujarati by the poet and Adil Jussawala, used by permission of Gulammohamed Sheikh and Adil Jussawala.

'Kabariwala' by Kavita A. Jindal, used by permission of Kavita A. Jindal.

'Kalli' by Ajmer Rode, translated from Punjabi by the poet, first published at Poetry International Web, Rotterdam, used by permission of Ajmer Rode.

'Lamination' by Shefali Debbarma, translated from Kokborok by Saroj Chaudhuri, reworked by Abhay K., used by permission of Shefali Debbarma, Saroj Chaudhuri and Abhay K.

'Let Loose the Stinging Bees' by Kanji Patel, translated from Gujarati by Gopika Jadeja, used by permission of Gopika Jadeja.

'Lineage' by Attoor Raviverma, translated from Malayalam by K. Satchidanandan, used by permission of Attoor Raviverma and K. Satchidanandan.

'Love is Everyday New and Fresh' by Bulleh Shah, translated from Punjabi by K.S. Duggal.

'Love Song' by Nirala, translated from Hindi by Arvind Krishna Mehrotra, used by permission of Arvind Krishna Mehrotra.

'Magadh' by Srikant Verma, translated from Hindi by Mrinal Pande, used by permission of Mrinal Pande.

'Making a Chair' by Dileep Jhaveri, used by permission of Dileep Jhaveri.

'Making Love to Her' by Dharmakirti from *Subhashit Ratnakosha* (477), translated from Sanskrit by Abhay K., used by permission of Abhay K.

'Married Love' by Srinivas Rayaprol, used by permission of Aparna Rayaprol.

'Meditations on Desire' by Saleem Peeradina, used by permission of Saleem Peeradina.

'Moment' by Kaifi Azami, translated from Urdu by Pavan K. Varma, used by permission of Pavan K. Varma.

'Momin' by Kailash Vajpeyi, translated from Hindi by Ananya Vajpeyi, used by permission of Ananya Vajpeyi.

'Monsoon Clouds Be My Messenger' by Andal, translated from Old Tamil by Priya Sarukkai Chhabria, used by permission of Priya Sarukkai Chhabria.

'Monsoon Poem' by Tishani Doshi, first published in *Girls are Coming out of the Woods* (Harper Collins), used by permission of Tishani Doshi.

'Mother Tongue' by Kedarnath Singh, translated from Hindi by Kalpana Singh-Chitnis, used by permission of Kedarnath Singh and Kalpana Singh-Chitnis.

'Mountain Child' by Nirmala Putul, translated from Hindi by Lucy Rosenstein, used by permission of Lucy Rosenstein.

'My Eight-anna Coin' by Vinod Kumar Shukla, translated from Hindi by Arvind Krishna Mehrotra, used by permission of Vinod Kumar Shukla and Arvind Krishna Mehrotra.

'My Poem' by Surjit Patar, translated from Punjabi by Nirupama Dutt, used by permission of Surjit Patar and Nirupama Dutt.

'My Sister's Bible' by S. Joseph, translated from Malayalam by K. Satchidanandan, used by permission of S. Joseph and K. Satchidanandan.

'Need' by Ramesh Chandra Shah, translated from Hindi by the poet.

'Negro, My Brother' by Ali Sardar Jafri, translated from Urdu by Baider Bakht and Kathleen Grant Jaeger.

'Night's Golden Wineglasses' by Habba Khatoon, transcreated from Kashmiri by Abhay K. and Bill Wolak, used by permission of Abhay K. and Bill Wolak.

'No, I Am not Losing My Sleep' by Pash, translated from Punjabi by Suresh Sethi.

'Not Entirely Hidden' from *Cātu* verses, translated from Telugu by Velcheru Narayana Rao and David Shulman, used by permission of Velcheru Narayana Rao and David Shulman.

'O My Friends' by Mirabai, transcreation (c) Jane Hirshfield; used by permission of Jane Hirshfield. First appeared in Women in Praise of the Sacred: 43 Centuries of Spiritual Poetry by Women, ed. by Jane Hirshfield (NY: HarperCollins, 1994) and Mirabai: Ecstatic Poems, ed. by Robert Bly and Jane Hirshfield (Boston: Beacon Press, 2004).

'O Sakhi, the Flute Plays in the Grove' by Salabega, translated from Oriya by Sachidanand Mohanty and Smita Mohanty, used by permission of Sachidanand Mohanty.

'Only a Connoisseur' by Anon.

'Only One Face' by Pankaj Chaturvedi, translated from Hindi by Rahul Soni, used by permission of Pankaj Chaturvedi and Rahul Soni.

'Pataliputra' by Patumarattu Mocikiranar, Indian Literature, 39.1 (January-February 1996) translated from Tamil by R. Parthasarathy, copyright © 2017 by R. Parthasarathy, used by permission of R. Parthasarathy.

'Paths' by Salma, translated from Tamil by Lakshmi Holmström, used by permission of Salma, Mark Holmström and Radhika Holmström.

'Pedru Uncle' by Hemant Divate, translated from Marathi by Dilip Chitre, used by permission of Hemant Divate and Vijaya Chitre.

'People' by Tukaram, translated from Marathi by Anon.

'Pigeons' by Bibhu Padhi, used by permission of Bibhu Padhi.

'Play' by Ashok Vajpeyi, translated from Hindi by Sudeep Sen, used by permission of Ashok Vajpeyi and Sudeep Sen.

'Portrait' by Dinkar Manwar, translated from Marathi by Sachin Ketkar, used by permission of Dinkar Manwar and Sachin Ketkar.

'Praise Galore to the Land of Dhat' by Rangrelo Bithu, translated from Rajasthani by Kesari Singh.

'Prayer' by Prabodh Parikh, translated from Gujarati by Naushil Mehta and Ranjit Hoskote, used by permission of Prabodh Parikh and Ranjit Hoskote.

'Pundarīka' by Kshemendra, translated from Sanskrit by W.S. Merwin and J.M. Masson, used by permission of J.M. Masson.

Rāghavapāṇḍavīya 1.47 by Kavirāja, transcreated from Sanskrit by Gabriel Rosenstock and Abhay K., used by permission of Gabriel Rosenstock and Abhay K.

'Rumi and the Reed' by Tabish Khair, used by permission of Tabish Khair.

'Satyabhama' by Basudev Sunani, translated from Odia by Rabindra K. Swain, used by permission of Basudev Sunani and Rabindra K. Swain.

Selections from *Amaruśataka*, transcreated from Sanskrit by Gabriel Rosenstock and Abhay K., used by permission of Gabriel Rosenstock and Abhay K.

Selections from *Chauraspanchasika* by Bilhana, a free interpretation of the *Chauraspanchasika* (Sanskrit) by E. Powys Mathers. Available in public domain.

Selections from *Gathasaptasati*, translated from Maharashtri Prakrit by Arvind Krishna Mehrotra. The numbers following the poems are according to Albrecht Weber's Das Saptacatakam des Hala (Leipzig: F.A. Brockhaus, 1881). Used by permission of Arvind Krishna Mehrotra.

Selections from *The Rigveda and The Upanishadas* – 'Gayatri Mantra' translated from Sanskrit by Swami Vivekananda, available in public domain; 'Pavamāna Mantra' (from *Bṛhadāraṇyaka Upaniṣad*), 'Shanti Mantra' (from *Bṛhadāraṇyaka Upaniṣad*), 'Vasudhaiva Kutumbakam' (From *Maha Upanisad*), translated from Sanskrit by Abhay K., used by permission of Abhay K.

Selection from *Saduktikarṇāmṛta* by Śrīdharadāsa, transcreated from Sanskrit by Gabriel Rosenstock and Abhay K., used by permission of Gabriel Rosenstock and Abhay K.

Selection from *Śārṅgadharapaddhati* by Śārṅgadhara, transcreated from Sanskrit by Gabriel Rosenstock and Abhay K., used by permission of Gabriel Rosenstock and Abhay K.

Selections from *Subhāṣitaratnakoṣa* 815 (24.9) by Silabhattarika and 1614 (48.21) by Śilhana, transcreated from Sanskrit by Gabriel Rosenstock, used by permission of Gabriel Rosenstock.

Selection from *Subhāṣitāvalī* by Vallabhadeva, transcreated from Sanskrit by Gabriel Rosenstock and Abhay K., used by permission of Gabriel Rosenstock and Abhay K.

Selections from *Therigatha*, poems of Mutta and Sumangalmata, transcreation by Abhay K. and Gabriel Rosenstock, original language: Pali, used by permission of Abhay K. and Gabriel Rosenstock.

'Shadow' by Brij Nath Betab, translated from Kashmiri by the poet, used by permission of Brij Nath Betab.

'Shapes' by Chokhamela, translated from Marathi by Rohini Mokashi-Punekar, used by permission of Rohini Mokashi-Punekar.

'Silhouette' by Adil Jussawala, used by permission of Adil Jussawala.

'Sita's Tears' by Udayan Vajpeyi, translated from Hindi by Alok Bhalla, used by permission of Alok Bhalla.

'Son to Mother' by Gnanakoothan, translated from Tamil by Ashokamitran.

'Song of the Avadhut' by Dattatreya, translated from Sanskrit by S. Abhayananda, used by permission of S. Abhayananda.

'Soul Song' by Abhay K., used by permission of Abhay K.

'Summer' from *Vajjalagam* of Jayabhallava, translated from Prakrit by Martha Ann Selby, used by permission of Martha Ann Selby.

'Summer Afternoon' by Vijay Deo Narayan Shahi, translated from Hindi by Arvind Krishna Mehrotra, used by permission of Arvind Krishna Mehrotra.

'Sundori' by Kynpham Sing Nongkynrih, translated from Khasi by the poet, used by permission of Kynpham Sing Nongkynrih.

'Terms of Seeing' by E.V. Ramakrishnan, used by permission of E.V. Ramakrishnan.

'The Art of Courtesan' by Anon, translated from Malayalam by P. Narayana.

'The Battlefield' (Purananuru 278) by Kakkaipatiniyar Naccellaiyar, translated from Tamil by R. Parthasarathy, used by permission of R. Parthasarathy.

'The Black Man' by Ved Pal Deep, translated from Dogri by Balraj Puri.

'The Corpse' by J.P. Das, translated from Odia by Jayanta Mahapatra, used by permission of J.P. Das and Jayanata Mahapatra.

'The Cowherd's Daughter' by Rūpa Gosvāmin, translated from Sanskrit by W. S. Merwin & J.M. Masson, used by permission of J.M. Masson.

'The Day She Was Gone' by Namdeo Dhasal, translated from Marathi by Dilip Chitre. Used by permission of Vijaya Chitre.

'The Description of Uma's Lovemaking' by Kalidasa, transcreated from Sanskrit by Abhay K., used by permission of Abhay K.

'The Difference' by Akhtar-ul-Iman, transcreated from Urdu by Abhay K. and Bill Wolak, used by permission of Abhay K. and Bill Wolak.

'The Door' by Anamika, translated from Hindi by Ritu Menon, used by permission of Anamika.

'The Evening' by Garikapati Pavan Kumar, translated from Telugu by D. Kesava Rao.

'The Glow-Worm's Gleam' by Narain Shyam, translated from Sindhi by D.K. Mansharamani.

'The Heron' by Nannakaiyar, *Modern Poetry in Translation*, New Series, 9 (Summer 1996), translated from Tamil by R. Parthasarathy. Copyright © 2017 by R. Parthasarathy, used by permission of R. Parthasarathy.

'The Insane' by Vinda Karandikar, translated from Marathi by the poet.

'The Leaf on the Branch' by Gulzar, translated from Urdu by Pavan K. Varma, used by permission of Gulzar and Pavan K. Varma.

'The Magician' by Kamal Vora, translated from Gujarati by Dileep Jhaveri and Bill Wolak, used by permission of Kamal Vora, Dileep Jhaveri and Bill Wolak.

'The Messenger Speaks to Radha' by Jayadeva, translated by Andrew Schelling (from *The Gita-govinda* in Kamini: Poems from Jayadeva's *Gita-govinda*—emdash editions: St. Louis, 2007), used by permission of Andrew Schelling.

'The Need to Travel' by Sohini Basak, used by permission of Sohini Basak.

'The New Man' by Anon Baul.

'The Orientalist' by Ranjit Hoskote, first published in Ranjit Hoskote, *Vanishing Acts: New & Selected Poems 1985-2005* (New Delhi: Penguin, 2006) used by permission of Ranjit Hoskote.

'The Sea' by Sitanshu Yashaschandra, translated from by E.V. Ramakrishnan, used by permission of Sitanshu Yashaschandra and E.V. Ramakrishnan.

'The Secret' by Joseph Furtado. Available in public domain.

'The Sleep' by Sankha Ghosh, translated from Bengali by Kalyan Roy.

'The Taste of Iron' by Dhumil, translated from Hindi by Kamalakar Bhat, used by permission of Kamalakar Bhat.

'The Tiger' by Kavarpentu (*Purananuru 86*), *Modern Poetry in Translation*, New Series, 9 (Summer 1996). Translated from Tamil by R. Parthasarathy. Copyright © 2017 by R. Parthasarathy, used by permission of R. Parthasarathy.

'The Unicorn' by Suniti Namjoshi from *Poems* (Writers' Workshop, 1967), used by permission of Suniti Namjoshi.

'The Way' by Bodhidharma, transcreated from Sanskrit by Gabriel Rosenstock, used by permission of Gabriel Rosenstock.

'The Yellow Mustard' by Amir Khusrau, translated by Anon, available in public domain.

'The Young Woman Who Sells Flowers' by Parimal Hansda, translated from Santhali by Hansda Sowvendra Shekhar, used by permission of Parimal Hansda and Hansda Sowvendra Shekhar.

'They Burnt My Father and Grandfather' by K. Siva Reddy, translated from Telugu by M. Sridhar and Alladi Uma, used by permission of K. Siva Reddy, M. Sridhar and Alladi Uma.

'Things of Beauty' by Amrita Nair, used by permission of Amrita Nair.

'Thirst' by Sahir Ludhianvi, transcreated from Urdu by Gabriel Rosenstock, used by permission of Gabriel Rosenstock.

'This Helplessness' by Shamsher Bahadur Singh, translated from Hindi by Nalini Taneja, used by permission of Nalini Taneja.

'Tibet' by Uday Prakash, translated from Hindi by Robert A. Hueckstedt, used by permission of Uday Prakash and Robert A. Hueckstedt.

'Time' by Kambadasan, translated from Tamil by N.V. Rajamani.

'Time Does Not Pass' by Rajendra Bhandari, translated from Nepali by Anmole Prasad, used by permission of Rajendra Bhandari and Anmole Prasad.

'To Her Besties' by Vidyā, translated from Sanskrit by Abhay K., used by permission of Abhay K.

'Traffic Jam' by Nilim Kumar, translated from Assamese by Bibekanand Choudhury, used by permission of Nilim Kumar.

'Wasn't It Woman Who Bore Them' by Sanchiya Honnamma, translated from Kannada by Tejaswini Niranjana, used by permission of Tejaswini Niranjana.

'What Blue Is' by Binoy Majumdar from *Come Back Wheel (No. 70)*, translated from Bengali by Arunava Sinha, used by permission of Arunava Sinha.

'What Frenzy is this?' by Zareef Ahmed Zareef, translated from Kashmiri by the poet, used by permission of Zareef Ahmed Zareef.

'When it Rains in Dharamshala' by Tenzin Tsundue, used by permission of Tenzin Tsundue.

'When You Come' by Anupama Basumatary, translated from Assamese by Pradip Acharya, used by permission of Anupama Basumatary.

'Where the Mind Is Without Fear' by Rabindranath Tagore, translated from Bengali by the poet, available in public domain.

'While I Slept' by Navtej Bharati translated from Punjabi by the poet, used with the permission of the poet

'Whirlwind' by Ravji Patel translated from Gujarati by Hansa Jhaveri.

'Who Was It' by Shahryar, translated from Urdu by Rakhshanda Jalil, used by permission of Rakhshanda Jalil.

'Why Marry' by Vemana, transcreated from Telugu by Amanda Bell, used by permission of Amanda Bell.

'Winter' by Bijoy Sankar Barman, translated from Assamese by Narendra Nath Thakuria, used by permission of Bijoy Sankar Barman and Narendra Nath Thakuria.

'Within' by Basavanna, translated from Kannada by Laxmi Chandrashekar and Vijaya Guttal, reworked by Gabriel Rosenstock, used by permission of Laxmi Chandrashekar , Vijaya Guttal and Gabriel Rosenstock.

'Without My Body' by B.B. Agarwal, translated from Hindi by Abhay K., used by permission of Abhay K.

'You' by Ismail, translated from Telugu by Velcheru Narayan Rao, used by permission of Velcheru Narayan Rao.

'You and I' (*Kuruntokai 40*), translated from Tamil by George L. Hart, used by permission of George L. Hart.

'You are That' from *Chhandogya Upanishad*, translated from Sanskrit by Swami Purohit and W.B. Yeats, in public domain.

'You Cannot Own Someone' by Firaq Gorakhpuri, translated from Urdu by the poet.

'You Would Have Been a Saint' by Ghalib, translated from Urdu by Gulzar, used by permission of Gulzar.

'Your Thoughts' by Raghuvir Sahay, transcreated from Hindi by Amanda Bell, used by permission of Amanda Bell.

'Your Trust' by Om Nagar translated from Rajasthani by Abhay K. used by permission of Om Nagar and Abhay K.

ABOUT THE POETS

Abhay K. (b. 1980) has published seven collections of poetry including *The Seduction of Delhi*, *The Eight-eyed Lord of Kathmandu* and *The Prophecy of Brasilia*. He is also the editor of *CAPITALS* and *New Brazilian Poems*.

Adil Jussawala (b. 1940) is the author of four books of poems. His third book, *Trying to Say Goodbye*, was given a Sahitya Akademi award in 2014. He has been a language teacher, a lecturer, and literary editor and columnist for several newspapers and magazines.

Agyeya is the pen name of Sachchidananda Hirananda Vatsyayan (1911–1987). He introduced modern trends in Hindi poetry, fiction, criticism and journalism. He was an exponent of the literary movements *Nayi Kavita* (New Poetry) and *Prayog* (Experiments) in Modern Hindi literature.

Ajmer Rode (b. 1940) is a poet, playwright and translator with five volumes of poetry to his credit. He lives in Canada and writes in Punjabi and English.

Akhtar-ul-Iman (1915–1996) is a poet, scholar, film script writer and director. He wrote in Urdu, published eight collections of poetry and received Sahitya Akademi Award.

Ali Sardar Jafri (1913–2000) is a prolific and versatile Urdu writer, poet, critic and film lyricist. He received Jnanpith Award in 1997 and Padma Shri in 1967.

Alok Dhanwa (b. 1948) is poet from Munger, Bihar who has been active in the left cultural movement since decades. He has two poetry collections to his credit. He has received several awards including Rahul Samman and Bihar Rashtrabhasa Parishad Award.

Amir Khusrau (1253-1325) is a Sufi musician, poet and scholar. He is an iconic figure in the cultural history of the Indian subcontinent. He was a mystic and a spiritual disciple of Nizamuddin Auliya of Delhi. He wrote poetry primarily in Persian, but also in Hindavi.

Amit Majmudar (b. 1979) is poet and novelist, translator, essayist, and diagnostic nuclear radiologist (M.D.) who lives in Ohio, USA. His latest book is *Godsong*: A Verse Translation of the *Bhagvad-Gita* with commentary.

Amrita V. Nair (b. 1989) is a writer based in Singapore. Her first collection of poetry, *Yours Affectionately*, was published in 2009 and received the Jury's commendation at the Muse India National Literary Awards 2011.

Anamika (b. 1961) is a contemporary Hindi poet, social worker and novelist from Bihar. She also writes literary criticism in English.

Andal is the only woman among the twelve Alvar saints of South India affiliated to the Srivaishnava tradition of Hinduism. Active in the 7-8th century, she is credited with the great Tamil works *Thiruppavai* and *Nachiar Tirumozhi*.

Angshuman Kar (b. 1975) is the author of nine collections of poems, two novels, two novellas and a memoir. He received several awards, including the Krittibas Award in 2007.

Anitha Thampi (b. 1968) writes in Malayalam and has published two poetry collections. Her poems have been translated into several languages.

Annamayya (1408–1503) is a Hindu saint and the earliest known Indian musician to compose songs called *sankirtanas* in praise of the god Venkateswara, a form of Vishnu.

Anupama Basumatary (b.1961) has five collections of poetry and a book of translation to her credit. She received the Bharatiya Bhasha Parishad's Ishan Award for her book *Rupali Ratir Ghat*.

Anuradha Mahapatra (b. 1957) is a poet, writer and social activist. She writes in Bengali. She has published four collections of poems and two collections of essays.

Arvind Krishna Mehrotra (b.1947) is a poet, anthologist, literary critic and translator. He is widely recognized for expanding the Indian English language poetry tradition, established by figures such as A.K. Ramanujan, Nissim Ezekiel, Dom Moraes and Arun Kolatkar.

Ashok Vajpeyi (b. 1941) is a poet, essayist, literary and cultural critic. He writes in Hindi. He has published 23 books of poetry, criticism and art. He received Sahitya Akademi Award in 1994.

Attoor Ravi Varma (1930-2019) is one of the pioneers of modern Malayalam poetry, who has won the Kendriya Sahitya Akademi Award for his contributions to literary world.

Basavanna is a 12th century Hindu philosopher, statesman, Kannada poet in the Shiva-focused Bhakti movement and a social reformer.

He is known to have spread social awareness through his *Vachanas*, a specific rhythmic writing in Kannada.

Basudev Sunani (b. 1962) is the author of four poetry collections. He is considered as a significant Dalit voice in Odia poetry.

B.B. Agarwal (1919–1975) is an important figure in *Pragativad* movement of Hindi poetry. He published nine collections of poetry and was awarded Sahitya Akademi Award posthumously.

Bhavabhuti is an 8th century scholar of India, noted for his plays and poetry, written in Sanskrit. His play *Malati Madhava* is considered a masterpiece in Sanskrit literature.

Bhojya Deva is a well-known 11th century poet, patron of poets and King of Dhara.

Bibhu Padhi (b. 1951) has published eleven books of poetry. His poems have appeared in distinguished magazines and anthologies throughout the English-speaking world.

Bijoy Sankar Barman (b. 1980) is an Assamese poet and translator with ten published books to his credit. He received Sahitya Akademi Yuva Puraskar in 2013 among other awards.

Bilhana is an 11th century Kashmiri poet. He is known for his love poem, the *Chauraspanchasika* or *The Love Thief*.

Binoy Majumdar (1934–2006) is a prominent Bengali poet. He published seven poetry collections and received several awards including the Sahitya Akademi Award in 2005.

Bodhidharma (5th-6th century CE) is a Buddhist monk traditionally credited as the transmitter of Chan Buddhism to China. According to Chinese legend, he also began the physical training of the monks of Shaolin Monastery creating Shaolin kungfu.

Brij Nath Betab (b. 1953) is a renowned Kashmiri poet and an important voice in Kashmiri poetry in post independent India. His poems sing the pain of exile from the homeland. He has been honoured with several awards including Delhi State Urdu Academy Award.

Buddhadev Bose (1908–1974) is a major voice in Bengali literature. He wrote novels, short stories, plays and essays in addition to poetry. He received Sahitya Akademi Award in 1967 and Padma Bhusan in 1970.

Bulleh Shah (1680–1757) is a Punjabi poet and philosopher. His first spiritual teacher was Shah Inayat Qadiri, a Sufi murshid of Lahore.

The verse form Bulleh Shah primarily employed is the Kafi, popular in Punjabi (Saraiki) and Sindhi poetry.

Chokhamela is one of the first Dalit poets of India from the 14th century. He is revered as a saint in Maharashtra. He belonged to the Mahar caste, which was considered untouchable in that era. He wrote many *Abhangas*, a form of devotional poetry sung in the praise of god Vitthala/Vithoba.

Dattatreya is a poet who is also considered as an incarnation of the Divine Trinity – Brahma, Vishnu and Shiva – in Hindu mythology.

Debjani Chatterjee (b. 1952) is a poet based in UK. She has written, translated, or edited more than 60 books. She was honoured with an MBE in 2008.

Devara Dasimaya is a 10th century poet who wrote in Kannada. He composed *vachanas* in the name of his god Ramnath.

Dharmakriti is an influential Indian Buddhist philosopher. He was active in the 6-7th century. He worked at Nalanda and was one of the key scholars of epistemology (pramana) in Buddhist philosophy.

Dhumil (1936–1975) is a renowned Hindi poet from Varanasi, who is known for his revolutionary writings and "protest poetry". His posthumously released second collection of poems earned him Sahitya Akademi Award in 1979.

Dileep Jhaveri (b. 1943) is a Gujarati language poet, translator, playwright, editor and physician from Mumbai. He has published three poetry collections in Gujarati and has edited an anthology of contemporary Gujarati poetry in English translation entitled *Breath Becoming a Word*.

Dilip Chitre (1938–2009) is one of the foremost poets and critics to emerge in the post-independence period of India. Apart from being a very important bilingual writer in Marathi and English, he was also a painter and filmmaker.

Dinkar Manwar (b. 1965) is a poet, editor and artist from Maharashtra, India. His poems have been published in various literary journals and he has two poetry collections to his credit.

E.V. Ramakrishnan (1950) is a bilingual writer and translator. He has published poetry and literary criticism in Malayalam, his mother tongue and English. He has three volumes of poetry in English and five critical books in Malayalam. He received Kerala Sahitya Akademi Award.

Eunice de Souza (1940–2017) is an English language poet, literary critic and novelist. Among her notable books of poetry are *Fix* and *Women in Dutch Painting* (1988).

Firaq Gorakhpuri (1896–1982) is the pen name of Raghupati Sahay, a writer, critic and one of the most noted contemporary Urdu poets from India. He received Jnanpith Award in 1969 for his magnum opus *Gul-e-Naghma*.

G.S. Sharat Chandra (1935–2000) is an author of both poetry and fiction. Much of his work touches on the deep emotions of the Indian/American immigrant. His most famous work *Family of Mirrors* was a 1993 Pulitzer Prize nominee for poetry.

Gagan Gill (b. 1959) has published four collections of poetry. She has also published ten volumes of translations.

Garikapati Pavan Kumar (b. 1972) is a poet and a translator. He has translated poems of Pablo Neruda into Telugu. His first book of poems in Telugu received Ismail Award. He lives in the United States.

Ghalib (1797–1869) is the pen name of Mirza Asadullah Beg Khan. He was a preeminent Urdu and Persian-language poet during the last years of the Mughal Empire.

Gopal Honnalgere (1942–2003) is a prominent Indian English poet with six poetry collections to his credit.

Gulam Mohammed Sheikh (1937) is a painter, poet and art critic from Gujarat. He was awarded the Padmashri in 1983 and Padmabhushan in 2014 for his contribution in the field of art.

Gulzar (b. 1934) is the pen name of Sampooran Singh Kalra. He is a well-known poet, lyricist and film director. He received the Sahitya Akademi Award in 2002 for his short stories collection *Dhuan*.

H.S. Shivaprakash (b. 1954) is a leading Kannada poet and playwright. He has several published anthologies of poems and plays to his credit. He received Sahitya Akademi Award in 2012.

Habba Khatun (1554–1609) is a 16th century poet and ascetic, who is also known as the 'Nightingale of Kashmir'. She is a legendary figure in Kashmiri literary history.

Hemant Divate (b. 1967) is a reputed Marathi poet, editor, translator and publisher based in Mumbai. He has published several poetry collections.

Hoshang Merchant (b. 1947) is a poet based in Hyderabad who writes in English. He has written 20 books of poetry, and four critical studies. He edited India's first gay anthology *Yaraana: Gay Writing from India*.

J.P. Das (b. 1936) is a well-known poet, fiction writer and playwright from Odisha. He is the winner of many honours including the Sahitya Akademi Award and the Saraswati Samman.

Janabai is a 14th century Marathi poet. She is traditionally attributed with the authorship of about 300 *abhangas*. She is revered as a saint by the followers of Warakari sect in Maharashtra.

Jayadeva (1170–1245) is a Sanskrit poet known for his epic poem *Gita Govinda* which concentrates on Krishna's love with Radha in spring season.

Jayanta Mahapatra (b. 1928) is one of the best known contemporary poets and the first ever Indian poet to win the Sahitya Akademi award for English poetry.

Jayavallabha is an 8th century Jain monk. He is known for compiling *Vajjalagan*, a collection of verses in Prakrit.

Jiban Narah (b. 1970) is the author of six books of poetry in Assamese. His poems have been translated into many other languages.

Jibanananda Das (1899–1954) is a Bengali poet, writer, novelist and essayist. He is considered the most important voice in Bengali poetry after Tagore. During his lifetime, only seven volumes of his poems were published.

Jiwan Namdung (b. 1951) is one of the prominent literary figures in the contemporary Indian Nepali Literature. His significant work of criticism *Paryavekshan* won the Sahitya Akademi Award (1994).

Joseph Furtado (1872–1947) is a poet and novelist who wrote in the English language. Considered one of the best poets of Goa during his time, he is largely forgotten now.

K. Ayyappa Paniker (1930–2006) is an influential Malayalam poet, literary critic, and an academic and a scholar. He is one of the pioneers of modernism in Malayalam poetry.

K. Ramesh (b. 1966) writes haiku, tanka and free verse. His poems have appeared in several journals that cater to free verse and Japanese forms of poetry.

K. Satchidanandan (b. 1928) is a poet and critic. A pioneer of modern poetry in Malayalam, a bilingual literary critic, playwright, editor, columnist and translator, he writes in Malayalam and translates his poems into English.

K. Siva Reddy (b. 1943) is a significant voice in contemporary Telugu poetry. He has published eleven collections of poems and has won several awards including the Sahitya Akademi award in 1990.

K. Srilata (b. 1968) is a Chennai-based poet, fiction writer and translator. She writes in English. She has several publications to her credit.

Kabir is a 15th century mystic poet and saint. He ranks among the world's greatest poets. His writings influenced the Bhakti movement and his verses are found in Sikhism's scripture *Adi Granth*.

Kaifi Azami (1919–2002) is the pen name of Sayyid Akhtar Hussein Rizvi, a renowned Urdu poet and lyricist. He received the Sahitya Akademi Award in 1975 for his poetry collection *Awara Sajde*.

Kailash Vajpeyi (1936–2015) is a renowned Hindi poet. He received Sahitya Akademi Award in 2009 for his collection of poems *Hawa me Hastakshar*.

Kalidasa is a 5th century classical Sanskrit writer, widely regarded as the greatest poet and dramatist in the Sanskrit language. His plays and poetry are primarily based on the *Puranas*.

Kalpatta Narayanan (b. 1950) is a poet, essayist, novelist and a cultural activist. He writes in Malayalam.

Kamal Vora (b. 1950) is a Gujarati language poet and editor from Mumbai. He is the editor of *Etad*, a quarterly Guajarati literary magazine. He received the Sahitya Akademi Award in 2016.

Kambadasan (1916–1973) is an Indian writer, poet and popular film lyricist who worked mainly in Tamil-language films. He wrote several short stories, poems and plays.

Kaniyan Punkunran (1st–3rd Century CE) is an influential Tamil poet and philosopher of the Sangam age.

Kanji Patel (b. 1952) is a prominent poet-novelist of Gujarat. His published works revolve around folk and Adivasi communities and make use of the Adivasi language. His works have been widely translated.

Katyayani (b. 1959) is a poet, activist and publisher. She has published four collections of poems. Some of her poems have been translated into Russian and English.

Kavirāja is a 12th century Sanskrit poet famous for his double meaning poem, the *Rāghavapāṇḍavīya—Story of the Scion of Raghu and the Sons of Pāṇḍu*, the *Rāmāyaṇa* and the *Mahābhārata*.

Kavita A. Jindal (b. 1964) is the author of the poetry collection, *Raincheck Renewed*, published by Chameleon Press to critical acclaim. She has also published fiction, essays and reviews in newspapers and anthologies around the world.

Kedarnath Singh (b. 1934) is a poet, critic and essayist. He writes in Hindi. He was awarded India's highest literary award Jnanpith in 2013 and Sahitya Akademi Award in 1989.

Keki N. Daruwalla (b. 1937) is a poet and a short story writer in English. He was awarded Sahitya Akademi Award in 1984 for his poetry collection, *The Keeper of the Dead* and Commonwealth Prize for Asia for *Landscapes* in 1987.

Kshemendra (c. 990 – c. 1070 CE) is a Sanskrit poet from Kashmir. Around eighteen of his works are still extant while fourteen more are known only through references in other literature.

Kunwar Narain (1927-2017) writes in Hindi. Widely translated, his many honours include Sahitya Akademi Award, Italy's Premio Feronia, Warsaw University's honorary medal, Padma Bhushan and Jnanpith.

Kutti Revathi (b. 1974) is a lyricist, poet, activist and a doctor. She has published three books of poetry and is the editor of *Panikkudam*, a literary quarterly for women's writing.

Kynpham Sing Nongkynrih (b.1964) is a poet, translator and editor from northeast India. His poetry has been widely published in national and international journals. He writes in Khasi and English.

Lal Ded (1320–1392), known as Lalla, was a mystic. Her verses are the earliest compositions in Kashmiri language and are an important part in history of modern Kashmiri literature.

Mahe Jabeen (b. 1961) is a poet, lawyer and minority rights activist. Her poem features in the anthology *Hibiscus on the Lake: Twentieth-century Telugu Poetry from India* (University of Wisconsin Press).

Mangalesh Dabral (b. 1948) is a contemporary poet who writes in Hindi. He has published several collections of poetry and received the Sahitya Akademi Award in 2000.

Manohar Shetty (b. 1953) is a Goa-based poet who has eight books of poems to his credit and is one of the prominent Indian poets writing in the English language.

Manushya Puthiran (b. 1968) is the pen name of Tamil poet S. Abdul Hameed. He has several poetry collections to his credit.

Meena Alexander (1951–2018) is the author of numerous collections of poetry including *Atmospheric Embroidery* (2018). She has received several awards. She lives in New York City and is distinguished Professor of English at the Graduate Center/Hunter College, CUNY.

Mir Taqi Mir (1725–1810) was the leading Urdu poet of his time and one of the pioneers of the Urdu language. He was one of the key poets of the Delhi School of the Urdu ghazal.

Mirabai is a 16th century Hindu mystic poet and devotee of Krishna. She is a celebrated Bhakti saint, particularly in the North Indian Hindu tradition.

Mohammad Alvi (1927–2018) is a Urdu poet and the recipient of the Sahitya Akademi Award (1992). He published four collections of poems.

Mohammad Ismail (1928–2003) is a Telugu-language poet and critic. He was also an academic and university administrator. He wrote more than a dozen books including poetry, criticism and translations.

Muddupalani is an 18th century poet and courtesan. Her main works are the erotic epic *Rādhikā-sāntvanam* besides *Ashtapadi*, a Telugu translation of Jayadeva's eponymous work.

Munibur Rahman (b. 1924) has published nine books, including four poetry collections, beside several articles in scholarly journals. He lives in Michigan.

Mutta was an elder nun active around 600 BCE who contributed poems to one of first poetry anthologies in the world titled *Therigatha*.

N. N. Kakkad (1927–1987) is a poet in Malayalam language. He was a Sanskrit scholar as well as a broadcaster.

Nabaneeta Dev Sen (b. 1938) is an award-winning Indian poet, novelist and academic. She received Sahitya Akademi Award in 1999 and Padma Shri in 2000.

Nagarjuna (1911–1998) is the pen name of Vaidya Nath Mishra. He was a Hindi and Maithili poet, known as *Janakavi* – the People's Poet. He received the Sahitya Akademi Award in 1969.

Namdeo Dhasal (1949–2014) is a Marathi poet, writer and Dalit activist from Maharashtra, India. He won a Lifetime Achievement Award from the Sahitya Akademi in 2004.

Nannakaiyar (1st–3rd Century CE) is a Sangam era Tamil language poet.

Narain Shyam (1922–1989) is a prominent Sindhi poet. He published eleven collections of poetry. He received Sahitya Akademi Award in 1970.

Navtej Bharati (b. 1938) writes poetry and prose in Punjabi and English. His awards include Best Poet of the State (three times: 1959, 1960, 1961) by the Government of Punjab and the Anad Kav Sanman (Delhi, 2010). He lives in Canada.

Nida Fazli (1938–2016) is a prominent poet, lyricist and dialogue writer in Hindi and Urdu. He was awarded the Padma Shri in 2013 for his contribution to literature.

Nilim Kumar (b. 1961) has seventeen poetry collections and three novels to his credit. He writes in Assamese. His poems have been translated into several languages.

Nirala (1896-1961) [Suryakant Tripathi 'Nirala'] is a poet, novelist, essayist and story-writer and a prominent figure in modern Hindi literature.

Niranjan Chakma (b. 1951) has published eight collections of poetry. He received Ambedkar Fellowship Award in 1997. He lives in Agartala.

Nirmala Putul (b. 1972) writes in the Indian tribal language, Santali. A collection of her poems *Nagare Ki Tarah Bajte Hain Shabad* (Words resound like drums) was published in 2004. She counterpoises her tribal world with the 'developed' modern world.

Om Nagar (b. 1980) is the recipient of Sahitya Akademi's Yuva Purashkar 2012 for his collection of poems in Rajasthani. He has published four poetry collections. His poems have been translated into several Indian languages.

Padma Sachdev (b. 1940) is a poet and novelist. She is the first modern woman poet of the Dogri language. She also writes in Hindi and has published several poetry collections. She won the Sahitya Akademi Award in 1971.

Pankaj Chaturvedi (b. 1971) is a Hindi poet and critic. He has two poetry collections to his credit and has received Bharat Bhusan Samman Agrawal Samman and Devishankar Awasthi Samman.

Parimal Hansda (b. 1986) is a poet in Santhali language. He has published an anthology of poems and a collection of short stories.

Pash (1950–1988) is the pen name of Avtar Singh Sandhu. He was a major poet of the Naxalite movement in the Punjabi literature in 1970s.

Patumarattu Mocikiranar (1st–3rd Century CE) is a Sangam era Tamil language poet.

Pavankumar Jain (1947–2013) wrote in both English and Gujarati. His first collection of Gujarati poems, *Pasath Kavyo* (Sixty five poems), appeared in 2012.

R. Parthasarathy (b. 1934) is a poet, translator, and editor. He is best known for his long poem, *Rough Passage* (Oxford University Press, 1977). His translation of the Tamil epic, *The Tale of an Anklet* (Columbia University Press, 1993), received the Sahitya Akademi award in 1996.

Rabindranath Tagore (1861–1941) is the author of *Gitanjali*. He won the Nobel Prize in Literature in 1913.

Raghuvir Sahay (1929–1990) is a versatile Hindi poet, short-story writer, essayist, literary critic, translator, and journalist. He worked as the chief-editor of noted Hindi weekly, Dinmaan from 1969–82. He received the 1984 Sahitya Akademi Award.

Rajendra Bhandari (b. 1956) is a poet in Nepali. He has published several collections of poems.

Ramesh Chandra Shah (b. 1937) is a poet, novelist and critic. He received Sahitya Akademi Award for his novel, Vinayak in 2014. He was also conferred Padma Shri, the fourth highest Indian civilian award in 2004.

Rangrelo Bithu is a poet from Jaisalmer, Rajasthan who wrote in Rajasthani.

Ranjit Hoskote (b.1969) is the author of six collections of poetry. He has received the Sahitya Akademi Golden Jubilee Award, the Sahitya Akademi Translation Award, and the S H Raza Award for Literature.

Ravi Shankar (b. 1975) is an Indian American poet, editor, and former literature professor at Central Connecticut State University.

He received a Pushcart prize and has several collections of poetry to his credit.

Ravji Patel (1939–1968) is a poet, short story writer and novelist. He wrote in Gujarati. His only poetry collection *Angat* (1970) was published posthumously. It includes fourteen songs.

Rohan Chhetri (b. 1987) won 'Emerging Poets Prize 2015' for his first book of poems, *Slow Startle*. His poems have been published in several literary journals and have been translated into French. He was a 2016 Norman Mailer Poetry Fellow.

Rupa Goswamin (1489–1564) is a poet, philosopher and Guru of the Gaudiya Vaishnava tradition. He wrote a number of texts in Sanskrit on philosophy, poetics, drama and dramaturgy.

S. Joseph (b. 1965) writes in Malayalam. He received Kerala Sahitya Akademi Award in 2012. He has a number of poetry collections to his credit.

Sachal Sarmast (1739–1827) is the penname of Abdul Wahab Farouqi, a Sufi poet from Sindh. He wrote poetry in several languages, most prominently in Sindhi.

Sahir Ludhyanvi (1921-1980) is the pen name of poet and lyricist Abdul Hayee. He wrote in both in Hindi and Urdu. He won two Filmfare awards and received Padma Shri in 1971.

Salabega is a 17th century poet from Odisha. He occupies a permanent position among the devotional poets of Odisha for devoting his life to Lord Jagannath.

Saleem Peeradina (b. 1944) is the author of six books of poetry. He is an Emeritus Professor of English at Siena Heights University, Michigan, USA.

Salma (b. 1968) is a well-known name in contemporary Tamil literature. A poet, novelist and political activist, she has published two collections of poems, short fiction and novels.

Sampurna Chattarji (b. 1970) is a poet, novelist and translator. She has fourteen books to her credit including five poetry collections. Her translation of poems of Joy Goswami was shortlisted for inaugural Khushwant Singh Memorial Prize for Poetry.

Sankha Ghosh (b. 1932) writes in Bengali and has several collections of poems to his credit. He received Sahitya Akademi Award in 1977 and Jnanpith Award in 2016.

Śārṅgadhara is the 14th century compiler of Śārṅgadharapaddhati, a Sanskrit anthology (1363 CE) which has 4689 poetic verses divided into 163 sections (*paddhati*).

Shahryar (1936–2012) is a renowned poet and lyricist who was also an academician. He wrote in Urdu. He received the Sahitya Akademi Award in 1987 and Jnanpith in 2008.

Shakti Chattopadhyay (1933–1995) is a poet and writer in Bengali. He received the Sahitya Akademi Award in 1983.

Shankar Ramani (b. 1923) is a Goan poet felicitated with Sahitya Academy award for his poetry collection in Konkani in 1996.

Shakunt Mathur (b. 1922) is an experimental Hindi writer who contributed to New Poetry movement in Hindi literature in 1960–70s. She published three collections of poems.

Shamsher Bahadur Singh (1911–1993) was an important voice in progressive school of modern Hindi poetry. He published several poetry collections and received Sahitya Akademi Award in 1977 and Kabir Samman in 1989.

Shefali Debbarma (b. 1964) is poet from Tripura, northeast India. She writes in Kokborok. She received Tripura State Award for poetry in 2004.

Silabhattarika is a poet from ancient India known for grace and ease of her poetic style.

Silhana is a poet from Kashmir. His *Shantisataka* is quoted in *Saduktikarnamrta* which was composed in 1205 CE.

Sitanshu Yashaschandra (b. 1941) is a Gujarati poet, playwright, translator and academic. He received the Sahitya Akademi Award in 1987 and Padma Shri in 2006.

Sohini Basak's (b. 1991) debut collection of poems *we live in the newness of small differences* received the inaugural Beverley Manuscript Prize. She works as an editor at Harper Collins, India.

Souvik Bandyopadhyay (b. 1975) writes in Bengali. He has seven collections of poetry to his credit and has won several awards for poetry including the prestigious Mallika Sengupta Purashkar in 2017.

Śrīdharadāsa is a 12th century poet and compiler of Saduktikarṇāmṛta. He was active at the Sena court and is the author of various works in Sanskrit.

Srikant Verma (1931–1986) is a poet and the author of twenty books. He was also a politician. He was given the Sahitya Akademi Award posthumously for *Magadh*.

Srinivas Rayaprol (1925–1998) is a prominent Indian English poet. He also translated Telugu poetry into English. Three anthologies of his poetry were published by Writers Workshop, Kolkata.

Sumangalmata was an elder nun who lived around 600 BCE and contributed poems to one of first poetry anthologies in the world titled *Therigatha*.

Sumita Chakraborty (b. 1987) is poetry editor of AGNI Magazine. She received a Ruth Lilly and Dorothy Sargent Rosenberg Fellowship from the Poetry Foundation in 2017 and was shortlisted for the Forward Prize for Best Single Poem by the Forward Arts Foundation in 2018.

Sunil Gangopadhyay (1934–2012) is a poet and novelist who wrote in Bengali. He received Sahitya Akademi award in 1985 for his novel *Those Days* (*Sei Samaya*).

Suniti Namjoshi (b. 1941) is a poet and a fabulist. She has written many collections of fables and poetry, several novels, and more than a dozen children's books. Her work has been translated into several languages.

Surjit Patar (b. 1945) is a Punjabi language poet. He received the Sahitya Akademi Award in 1993.

Tabish Khair (b. 1966) is as associate professor at Aarhus University. Winner of the All India Poetry Prize, he is the author of several critically acclaimed novels and the poetry collections, *Where Parallel Lines Meet and Man of Glass*.

Tarannum Riyaz (b. 1953) is a noted Urdu fiction writer, critic, poet, essayist and translator. She has published several books. She received SAARC Literary Award 2014.

Tenetti Suri (1911–1958) is a prominent Telugu poet whose poems have been anthologized in *Hibiscus on the Lake: An Anthology of 20th century Telugu Poetry* edited by Velcheru Narayan Rao.

Tenzin Tsundue (b. 1975) is a poet, writer and an activist working for the Tibetan freedom movement. He has published four books. He won the first Outlook-Picador Award for Non-Fiction.

Tishani Doshi (b. 1975) is an award-winning poet, novelist and dancer. Her most recent book is *Girls Are Coming Out of the Woods. Small Days and Nights* is her forthcoming novel. She lives on a beach in Tamil Nadu with her husband and three dogs.

Tsering Wangmo Dhompa was born to Tibetan refugees in India (1969) and is now based in the US. She is the author of three poetry collections including *My Rice Tastes like the Lake* (2011) which was nominated for the Asian American Literary Awards. Her nonfiction book *A Home in Tibet* was published in 2014.

Tukaram is a 17th century poet-saint from Maharashtra, India. He is best known for his Abhanga, a form of devotional poetry sung in praise of the Hindu god Vitthala.

Uday Prakash (b. 1952) is a Hindi poet, scholar, journalist, translator and short story writer from India. He writes for major dailies and periodicals as a freelancer. He received SAARC Literary Award 2009.

Udayan Thakker (b. 1955) is a Gujarati language poet, writer and translator from Mumbai, India.

Udayan Vajpeyi (b. 1960) is a Hindi poet, essayist, script writer and translator. He has published two volumes of poetry, a short story collection, a book of essays and has received several awards.

Uttaran Chaudhuri (b. 1982) is a poet in Bengali. He works as a creative supervisor in an advertising firm in Kolkata. His poems have appeared in several literary magazines.

Vallabhadeva is a Sanskrit poet from the 16th century. He is one of the compliers of Subhasitavali.

Vallana is a well-known Sanskrit poet who is thought to have lived between the 9th and 10th century CE. Several of his poems appear in Vidyakara's poetry anthology *Subhashita Ratnakosa.*

Vasant Abaji Dahake (b. 1942) is a Marathi poet, playwright, short story writer, artist, and critic from Amaravati, Maharashtra. He received Sahitya Akademi Award in 2009 for his collection *Chitralipi.*

Ved Pal Deep (1929–1995) is a poet and translator. He wrote both in Hindi and Dogri.

Vemana is a 17th century Telugu poet. His poems are known for their use of simple language and native idioms. Vemana's poems were collected and published by C.P. Brown in the 19th century.

Vidya is among the foremost women poets in Sanskrit. Her verses have been included in *Subhashitaratnakosa* of Vidyakara, compiled in the 11th century CE.

Vidyapati (1352–1448) is a writer from Bihar who has written in Mathili and Sanskrit. His poetry influenced Bengali, Maithili, and other Eastern literary traditions.

Vijay Deo Narayan Shahi (1924–1982) is Hindi poet of repute. He is also known for his essays and literary criticism.

Vijay Seshadri (b. 1954) is a poet, essayist and literary critic. He won the 2014 Pulitzer Prize for poetry for *3 Sections*. His parents immigrated to the United States from Bangalore, India when he was five.

Vinda Karandikar (1918–2010) is a well-known Marathi poet, writer, literary critic, and translator. He translated his own poems into English. He received Jnanpith Award in 2003.

Vinod Kumar Shukla (b. 1937) is a prominent Hindi poet and novelist. He received Sahitya Akademi Award in 1999 for his novel *Deewar Mein Ek Khirkee Rahati Thi* (A Window lived in a Wall).

Vishwanath Prasad Tiwary (b. 1940) is a Hindi poet and critic. He has written a number of poetry books.

Yaquin (1727–1755) is a noted Urdu poet who was a rival of poet Mir Taqui Mir. He wrote poetry full of delicate and subtle romantic emotions. He was killed by his own father for unknown reasons.

Zareef Ahmed Zareef (b. 1943) writes poetry in Kashmiri. He has published four collections of poems. He is well-known for his satirical poems.

ABOUT THE TRANSLATORS

Abraham Thuruthumalil is a translator from Indian tribal languages.

Ajoy Ranjan Biswas is a poet and a well-known translator from Bengali into English. He retired as a Reader in English from Vivekanand College, Burdwan.

Alladi Uma taught at the University of Hyderabad for twenty years and is a well-known translator from Telugu into English.

Ananya Vajpeyi is an Indian academic and writer. She is the author of the award-winning book *Righteous Republic: The Political foundations of Modern India* (Harvard University Press).

Andrew Schelling is a poet, eco-activist, and translator from Sanskrit. He is the author of twenty odd books and teaches at Naropa University.

Anmole Prasad is a poet and translator. He translates from Nepali into English.

Apurva Narain translates from Hindi. His translations have been published in leading literary journals.

Arlene Zide is a poet and translator based in New York. She translates from Hindi and Urdu.

Arunava Sinha translates classic, modern and contemporary Bengali fiction, non-fiction and poetry from India and Bangladesh into English. Over forty of his translations have been published so far.

Arundhati Subramaniam is an award-winning poet and writer on spirituality and culture.

Arvind Krishna Mehrotra is a poet, anthologist, literary critic and translator. He is widely recognized for expanding the Indian English language poetry tradition.

Ashokamitran is the pen name of Jagadisa Thyagarajan, who is regarded as one of the most influential figure of Tamil lit of post-indepence era.

Balraj Puri (1928-2014) was a prolific writer in English as well as Urdu and Hindi. He was also a well-known journalist and human rights activist.

Bart Marshall is a well-known translator from Sanskrit into English. He has translated *Ashtavakra Gita* into English.

Bill Wolak is an American poet and translator. He teaches creative writing at William Paterson University in New Jersey.

Bibekanand Chaudhury is a noted translator of languages from the northeast India.

Bonnie MacDougall teaches at the University of Sydney and is a well-known translator.

C.S. Lakshmi is a writer and researcher. She writes under the pseudonym Ambai.

D. Kesava Rao is a well-known academic and translator from Telugu into English. His translations have appeared in several reputed literary journals.

D.K. Mansharamani is a noted translator. He translates from Sindhi into English.

David Shulman is an Indologist and regarded as one of the world's foremost authorities on the languages of India.

E. Powys Mathers (1892-1939) was an English translator and poet, known for his translation of *Asian Love Poems* and *One Thousand and One Nights*.

E.V. Ramakrishnan is a bilingual writer and translator. He has published poetry and literary criticism in his mother tongue Malayalam and in English.

Gabriel Rosenstock is a poet, tankaist, haikuist, novelist, essayist, playwright, author/translator of over 180 books, mostly in Irish (Gaelic).

George L. Hart is a professor of Tamil language at the University of California, Berkeley.

Gopika Jadeja is a bi-lingual poet and translator, writing in English and Gujarati. A recipient of the Charles Wallace Scholarship for Creative Writing, her poetry and translations have been published widely.

Hansda Sowvendra Shekhar is the author of two books. He translates from Santhali and Hindi into English.

Ivan M. Granger is the founder and editor of the Poetry Chaikhana, a publishing house and an online resource for sacred poetry from around the world.

J.M. Masson is an American author and translator. His translations of Sanskrit poems have received wide praise.

Jane Hirshfield is an award-winning American poet, essayist, and translator and author of several poetry collections.

Jas Yonjan 'Pyasi' is a poet and translator. He writes and translates from Nepali and Bengali.

Jayanta Mahapatra is one of the best known contemporary Indian English poets. He translates from Odia into English.

Kalpna Singh-Chitnis is an award-winning poet and translator. She translates from Hindi into English and vice versa. Her translated works have appeared in notable journals.

K. Satchidanandan is a poet and critic. A pioneer of modern poetry in Malayalam, a bilingual literary critic, playwright, editor, columnist and translator from Malayalam into English.

K.S. Duggal is a well-known writer of short stories, novels, dramas and plays. He received Sahitya Akademi Fellowship Award.

Kalyan Roy translates from Bengali into English.

Kamalakar Bhat is a bilingual writer and a translator between Kannada and English. He has translated poetry by several contemporary Kannada poets.

Kesari Singh is a translator of *Dingal* (Rajasthani) poetry into English. He is the editor of *An Anthology of Rajasthan Poetry*. He is also a politician and belongs to *Charan* community.

Laxmi Chandrashekhar is a prolific translator from Kannada into English.

Lakshmi Holmström (1935-2016) is a noted writer, literary critic and translator from Tamil.

Lucy Rosenstein teaches Hindi at SOAS, University of London. She grew up in Bulgaria.

Lyra Neog teaches English literature at Nowgong College, Assam and translates from Assamese into English.

M. Sridhar is former Professor at the Department of English Literature in the University of Hyderabad, India. He has published extensively in the areas of literary theory, comparative literature and translation.

Martha Ann Selby is an associate professor of South Asian studies in the Department of Asian Studies at the University of Texas at Austin, where she teaches courses on Indian literature.

Nabaneeta Dev Sen is an actor, writer, and child-rights activist. She studied literature at Harvard and has worked as a book editor, a screen writer, a short-film maker and a poetry translator.

Nalini Taneja is a professor at Delhi University. She translates from Hindi into English.

Narendranath Thakuria is a well-known translator from Assamese into English. His translations have appeared in Poetry International Web and leading literary journals.

Naushil Mehta is a well-known writer, producer and film director.

Neelav Bose is an occasional translator from Bengali into English.

Nirupama Dutt is a poet, translator, author and literary/art critic based in Chandigarh. Her latest translation includes Gulzar's short poetry collection Pluto.

Pavan K. Varma is a writer, translator, politician and former diplomat. He has authored several books.

Pradip Acharya has taught at Cotton College in Guwahati and is a prolific translator in Assamese and English.

R. Parthasarathy is a poet, translator, and editor. His translation of the Tamil epic, *The Tale of an Anklet* (Columbia University Press, 1993), received the Sahitya Akademi award in 1996.

Rabindra K. Swain has five books of poems to his credit. He translates from his mother tongue Odia. He is the managing editor of literary journal *Chandrabhaga*.

Rahul Soni is a well-known writer, translator and editor. He edited an anthology of Hindi Poetry in English translation and translated Shrikant Verma's collection of poetry *Magadh* among others.

Rakhsnanda Jalil is a writer, critic and literary historian. She has published over 15 books. She is presently writing a biography of Shahryar.

Ranjit Hoskote is a poet, cultural theorist and curator. He has authored 30 books. He was honoured with the Sahitya Akademi Award for translation.

Ritu Menon is a writer and publisher. She co-founded Kali for Women, India's first feminist publishing house.

Robert A. Hueckstedt teaches Hindi, Urdu and Sanskrit at the University of Virginia. His major interests are kavya, literature, literary theory, and translation.

Rohini Mokeshi-Punekar is professor of English at the Indian Institute of Technology, Guwahati.

Romila Thapar is a historian and author of several books. She has also translated some poetry, published in Poetry Chicago.

S. Abhayananda was born as Stanley Ross Trout in 1938 in Indianapolis, Indiana. He has authored and translated a number of books on spirituality including *The Avadhut Gita*.

Sachidanand Mohanty is a professor and Vice Chancellor of the Central University of Orissa, Koraput.

Sachin Ketkar is a bilingual writer, translator, editor, blogger and researcher based in Baroda, Gujarat. He won Indian Literature Poetry Translation Prize for translation of modern Gujarati poetry in 2000.

Saroj Chaudhury is a poet, academician and translator from tribal languages of North East India.

Sudeep Sen is a poet, editor and translator. His translations have featured in several reputed literary journals. He received A.K. Ramanujan Translation Award in 2009.

Sunita Jain is a scholar, novelist, short-story writer and poet of English and Hindi literature.

Suresh Sethi is a well-known translator from Punjabi into English. Several of his translations have appeared in *Indian Literature* and other reputed journals.

Tejaswini Niranjana is a professor, cultural theorist, translator and author.

Udayan Ghosh is a poet and translator from Assam. His translations have been published in several literary journals. He lives in Kolkata.

Velcheru Narayan Rao is a well-known translator from Telugu into English and a professor of Telugu Culture, Literature and History at Emory University, Atlanta, Georgia.

Vijaya Guttal is a retired professor of English from Karnatak University, Dharwad.

W.S. Merwin is a leading American writer whose poetry, translations, and prose have received accolades.

Disclaimer: Wikipedia is the principal source of the bio-notes of the late poets and translators included in this anthology. The bio-notes of most of the living poets and translators are provided by themselves.

POETS INDEX